TALK THE TALK

ACKNOWLEDGEMENTS

This book draws heavily on the wisdom of Carr Communications'
colleagues, notably Bunny Carr, Tom Savage, Anton Savage, Paul
McDonnell and Aoife Coonagh.

First published in 2007 by

CURRACH PRESS

55A Spruce Avenue, Stillorgan Industrial Park,

Blackrock, Co. Dublin

www.currach.ie

1 3 5 4 2

Cover by sin é design

Origination by Richard Parfrey

Printed by Betaprint, Bluebell Industrial Estate, Dublin 12

ISBN: 978-1- 85607-948-8

The author has asserted her moral rights

175555
€15

TALK THE TALK

TERRY PRONE

CURRACH
PRESS

For Bunny Carr,
best man, godfather, chief

Contents

1

It's the Communication, Stupid...

A surgeon saws the wrong leg off a patient.

A marriage splits up.

An applicant doesn't get a job for which they're more than qualified.

What went wrong?

The communication.

Someone didn't tell someone else.

Someone didn't listen.

Someone didn't convey the information they thought they were conveying.

Bad communication is at the root of every badly managed crisis, every unmet challenge, every corporate failure, every accident, every failed relationship.

That may sound like an exaggeration. It isn't.

Take 9/11.

Just four months before terrorists flew passenger jets into the Twin Towers, a swarthy young man turned up in a US Department of Agriculture office in Florida, looking for a loan. He wanted to buy a small crop-duster plane and fill the inside, except where the pilot sat, with an enormous tank. The idea made no sense to the loan officer, who turned down the application. The applicant then tried to buy – for cash – an aerial photograph of Washington D. C. hanging on the loan officer's wall. No dice on that one, either. But the conversation continued, unabated. How would the loan officer like it, the young man asked, if important buildings in her city were destroyed, the way buildings had been destroyed in the city the unsuccessful loan applicant came from? The loan officer, flummoxed, wondered how she'd get rid of this man, half-listening to him as he warbled on about an organisation that was going to change the face of the globe and its leader, Osama Bin Laden.

The loan officer half-listened to Mohammed Atta, one of the men who subsequently brought down the Twin Towers, because nobody had mentioned to her any suspicions about terrorist plans (although there were such suspicions). No radio or TV programme she'd watched had covered the threat of disaffected young male Muslims (although there was such a threat). No memo had landed on her desk warning her about the need to pass on any information she might glean from putative terrorists (and she had gleaned key information).

Breakdown in communication.

But it didn't stop there. Communication failures dogged and damned the response to the attacks that happened a few months later.

Minutes after the assault on the Twin Towers, when desperate workers within the stricken buildings climbed out on the windowsills, high above the ground, to escape the flames and smoke inside, the Battalion Chief of the Fire Department of New York used the public address system to try to calm them.

'Please don't jump,' he said into the microphone. 'We're coming up for you.'

Nobody heard him. The microphone was connected to nothing. The public address system had been destroyed. And while the chief knew his firefighters were slogging up the staircases in both towers, they were carrying outdated technology that didn't work well in high-rises.

Breakdown in communication because of technology failure.

And then there was the third instance. Firefighters were cut off from information that could have saved their lives. Those inside the tower had no idea that police helicopters had sent messages about how bad the situation was and predicting the collapse of the building they were in. They had no idea because the police ('New York's Finest') and the firefighters ('New York's Bravest') didn't actually get on that well together, didn't train together, and had no communications plan to allow speedy sharing of information in a crisis. Hundreds of firefighters perished when the towers collapsed.

Breakdown in communication because of failure to train people in cooperation and cross-disciplinary team-building.

The failures in communication during 9/11 were myriad, and each one of them caused immeasurable tragedy. They always do.

The worst air-traffic disaster in history, the 1976 crash in Tenerife between two fully loaded jumbo jets, resulted from communications breakdown. Between the control tower and the crew of a KLM plane on the ground. And between two members of that crew, sitting less than two feet away from each other.

What happened on the holiday island was that a security alert at Las Palmas airport caused the diversion of a number of flights to Tenerife. The single runway was overcrowded. A cloud came down, limiting visibility, and a Pan Am pilot didn't spot the exit from the runway he was supposed to take.

The air traffic controller, meanwhile, instructed the crew of a KLM flight to proceed to the runway and await further instructions.

At this point, a number of factors collided. The pilot of the KLM flight was fed up of the messing caused by the overcrowding at the airport. He knew that if his plane didn't take off quickly, he and his co-pilot would run out of flying time and would have to taxi back to the terminal and get the already tired passengers to disembark. He had been on the blower to air traffic control a number of times to get clarification about what was happening. He was an experienced pilot. An authoritative pilot.

So, when he misheard what had been said to him and started the moves for take-off, his co-pilot, who knew the runway wasn't clear, made only a hesitant croak, rather than the full-throated challenge which might have stopped the tragedy in which he himself died. He seems to have doubted the evidence of his own eyes: if so senior a captain believed it was safe to take off, well, it must be safe to take off...

The pilot told air traffic control, 'We are now at take-off,' but, because they weren't expecting him to take off, what they *heard* was him saying he was at take-off position. In fact, he was already moving. The KLM jumbo thundered down the runway and failed to clear the Pan Am plane. The death toll was horrific.

Communications breakdowns.

The kinds of breakdowns that happen in our daily lives are not always as obvious or dramatic. But they can damage careers, end relationships and destroy confidence. Good communication is central to happy and productive living. It's not an extra – it's the bloodstream of relationships and career progress. It doesn't matter how qualified you are or how hard you work, if you can't communicate, you're in trouble.

Keeping you out of trouble is what this book's about. You can dip into it at any point and find something useful or you can check out a topic in the Contents. Or you can decide, right now, how much you want to improve your communication skills, and use the book as a method to achieve that improvement.

You may want to improve your communication by 10 per cent or by 50 per cent. You may suffer from crippling shyness or from a nervousness that paralyses you when you have to make quite a routine presentation at work. You may have some event coming up – like a daughter's wedding – at which you fear you'll disgrace yourself and her by making a bad speech. You may be facing a crucial job interview. You may be a good communicator who wants to aim at excellence. Or you may have been reviewed – at work or at home – in a way that has devastated you and made you feel you need to hugely improve your communication skills.

Here's a promise. If you work through this book, practising the methods offered in the relevant sections until you have internalised them, made them a habit, a reflex, I guarantee that not only will you *radically* improve your communication skills, but that people will notice and comment on it. They may not say, 'You know, you were a rotten communicator up to now and you've improved a lot.' But they will mention how clear your presentation was or compliment you on the way you listen.

Why am I so sure you will improve measurably if you use this book? For two reasons.

The first is that everybody thinks they already know about communication. We do it all day, every day, after all. Of course we know how to do it. It's as natural as breathing. Isn't it?

To an extent, yes. Except that being familiar with something doesn't necessarily make you good at it. Emily Logan, the Ombudsman for Children, spends her life being lectured to by people who know exactly what she should do about every issue she has to address. They're certain – because they were once a child themselves. So they know.

Uh, uh. Human beings, including children, are individuals. Unique individuals, with unique needs, flaws, hopes, talents, dreams and disabilities.

Similarly, communicating the way you would to your best pal won't work if the person you must communicate with is a hostile boss who's made the decision that you're a waste of space. Nor will that method of communication work if you're a cancer specialist giving a difficult diagnosis to a patient. Whereas your friend knows you and is relaxed in your presence, your patient is already at a disadvantage because they know they're not well and have gone through tests. Their terror may inhibit their capacity to listen to what you're telling them. So you must adjust to the needs of the individual in the light of the situation.

If, on the other hand, you're curious about communication, about what works and doesn't work, you're way ahead of the majority of people. Which means your prognosis, as a communicator, is good.

The other reason I'm sure you'll improve is that, although this book sets out to be simple and enjoyable, it's based on solid research and on more than three decades of helping people find – and express – the best of themselves.

So let's start with the most important communication skill of all. The skill more than half the people you know don't have. The skill that's more absent than present, although its absence causes grief, misery and intense loneliness.

Good listening.

2

WE'RE ALL EARS

There's no such thing as conversation. It is an illusion.
There are intersecting monologues, that is all.

Dame Rebecca West (1892–1983)

'He never listens to me,' is the accusation that comes up, again and again, in marital quarrels. Wives make it about husbands. Husbands make it about wives.

Children rarely accuse their parents of not listening. But they could. Stand for fifteen minutes in a supermarket and watch toddlers and small children trying to attract parental attention in order to make a point or a request. You'll be startled by how poorly parents listen to their children.

As customers, most of us feel we're not listened to. Banks, building societies, department stores, hospitals and local authorities constantly find themselves under attack for failure to listen.

On the other side, when an organisation gets a great reputation with its customers or clients, that organisation's willingness to *listen* tends to be cited as one of the best things it has going for it.

Why are we such lousy listeners?

One of the reasons, in Ireland, is that we love talking and are good at it. If we could breed a bunch of people who would do nothing but listen attentively and make the occasional appreciative nod, we'd do it in a heartbeat. Our problem is that we can't get enough people to listen to us. No matter where you go, you find the intersecting monologues Rebecca West said we substitute for conversation.

That has consequences. Like loneliness and isolation. People slip through the meshes of our society because nobody listens to them. People end up paying (or having the state pay) for counselling in order to have someone hear them out. Counsellors do what good friends should do: shut up and listen. Listen. Ask questions. Feed back what they're hearing. And help the other person make their own decisions, not by suggesting options but by allowing the other person to talk out the possibilities without making judgements on one side or the other.

Becoming a good listener is the best step you can take, in communications terms. It can turn you into a better friend, a better family member, a better team member and a better boss. Improving no other communications skill can deliver so much.

The first step to becoming a great listener is a two-day talking detox.

It works this way.

For two days, you don't talk. No, you're not reduced to sign language. You're allowed to ask and answer questions. *If you really have to.* (And we'll come back to the kinds of questions that don't require an answer.) But other than essential answers to questions, you say not a thing for two days.

It may not sound like a huge challenge, but the few people who try it find it more difficult than the most rigorous diet.

Because the detox comes with a built-in condition. Other people must not notice you're not talking. This is not a freak-show, where the conversation around the water-cooler centres on whether you've been hit by a virus or joined a cult. You may not be talking, but you should be sustaining relationships while being silent. That means paying attention to people. Smiling at them. Touching them – if it's appropriate. Bringing them coffee. Laughing at their jokes.

If you do it well enough, most people won't notice that you're not talking. If, that is, you're a normal chatterbox like the rest of us. If you're normally an unstoppable monologuist, then of course people will notice. They may even assume you're sick. If they do, that just shows you how excessive your normal input is.

Within an hour on the first day, the payoffs begin. Instead of yelling up the stairs at a daughter to get out of the bathroom, you run up the stairs and knock on the bathroom door. Instead of asking a wife where a particular shirt is, you find it yourself. Instead of barking on about other drivers' misbehaviour, you get to hear the radio news. Instead of making phone calls to check up on details, you leave your colleagues un-nagged and give yourself thinking time.

At work, you will quickly learn that asking questions is like plugging in an appliance: it gets other people talking. Listen to them. If they're not interesting, *make* them interesting. One of your colleagues is complaining that her youngest is constantly getting infections at the playgroup she attends. Your instinct may be to say, 'Oh yes, it happened to mine all the time.' Stifle your instinct and just look surprised: 'Really?' Ask questions: How often? What kind? How bad? Infecting who else?

When someone arrives at your desk with a problem, put down whatever you're doing at the time. Move your face away from your computer screen and your hands away from the keyboard. Give the person your full, undivided attention while they talk.

The solution may be obvious to you. Don't state it. Question the other person until *they* come up with it. When they ask you what they should do, ask them what *they* think they should do. Keep the ball in their court and when they fix on the best action, warmly indicate approval. Nods, smiles and thumbs-up can, singly or together, convey the 'You've got it' message.

Of course, as the person walks away from your desk, you know you have a wealth of experience and anecdote based on similar problems in the past that you could have laid on them. But you will also know that your colleague will feel much better for simply coming up with their own solution and won't really miss hearing about how you rescued the company three years ago.

The kinds of questions that are useful, whether with an individual colleague or at a meeting, are not the accusatory questions like:

'Who did this?'

'How could this happen?'

'Have I not told you this was to be done this way?'

The best questions, not just to get other people talking, but to get them *thinking,* are the ones that help them reflect and analyse. Questions like:

'How bad/important is it?'
'Who are the key people involved?'
'Why do you think we have this problem?'
'How do you think we should tackle it?'
'What d'you think our options are?'
'And the best one?'
'How would that play out?'
'Any complicating factors?'
'Anything else we need to factor in?'
'Anyone else we should involve?'

What's important about those questions is that they're *inclusive.* Although you're getting the other person to talk, you're including yourself in their process by talking about 'our' problem and how 'we' can solve it.

Nor will you need that many questions. If you set out to find the other person or people interesting, that will be picked up by them, and they're more likely to feel free to tease out the issues and speculate about possible solutions.

When it's clear, with an individual, that they're plumping for one course of action, or, in the case of a meeting, that a consensus has built around one possible decision, don't yield to the temptation to announce it. Get *them* to announce it:

'So, summarise for me what we've decided...'

Even when asked for your opinion at a meeting, it's usually not just possible, but extremely productive, to seek permission to ask for clarification or elaboration of someone else's point. A gesture at the end of it may be enough to indicate, 'I'm with what he said.' If you must, in a formal business meeting, state your view, do it as briefly as possible and resume a positive silence.

A positive silence is a rare thing. One American writer accurately commented that for most people, the opposite to talking is not listening but waiting. Waiting impatiently to get one's own thoughts in. Too frequently, when silence is used, it is used negatively. A girlfriend may start giving a boyfriend the 'silent treatment'. Or a parent may employ a threatening silence as a way to evoke a confession or apology from their offspring.

That's unfortunate. Because silence, properly employed, can be more welcoming than an embrace. It can say, louder than words, 'I find you interesting. Please tell me more.' Silence is the great free gift that can be presented several times in any one day. It's a gift that enriches the giver as much as the receiver.

With children, silence can be more productive than questioning. Children, asked why they've done something, often get confused or frightened, because cause-and-effect are not clear to them. Nor is motivation. They just do things. Similarly, a visitor in a house who asks them what school they go to and what class they're in is a visitor most children want to get free of as quickly as possible.

Simply sitting down with children and letting them talk about whatever they want to talk about when they're good and ready to get started is much more productive. Research indicates that we harry children with questions and interruptions. They learn how to tell stories, give examples, master chronology by being listened to.

In addition, they find being listened to more rewarding than a handful of sweets. It makes them feel valued and important.

Someone once observed that we spend months celebrating the fact that a child has spoken its first words – and that we spend the next sixteen years telling the child to sit down and shut up. Listening to one's own children is one of the best services we can give them. (Reading to them runs it close, but that's for another book.)

At the end of the two-day talking detox, you will have made a number of advances. First and most important is the fact that you have broken the talking jag you may have been on for decades. You may not have completely broken it, but you're the best person to assess that. Mark yourself out of 10. Most people who do the detox

give themselves a 7 or an 8. Few hit a 9. A habit so engrained cannot
be eliminated in two days.

However, no matter where you mark yourself, you have taken
the first step towards becoming a truly great communicator. You
have begun to listen.

The next step is to train yourself to interview. All day. Every
day. For a week.

That requires amputation.

You have acquired, over the years, a wealth of offerings. Like:

- Jokes
- Family anecdotes
- Complaints
- Opinions
- Quotations from books
- Quotations from bosses, parents, children
- Facts
- Figures
- Observations

Try removing them from your communication for one week. It won't
be easy. But if, at the same time, you concentrate on interviewing the
people around you, it'll be a lot easier. Plus, you'll learn a plethora
of new jokes, family anecdotes, complaints, opinions, facts and
observations to refresh your existing stock.

We've already touched on the importance of questioning.

To move from amateur to professional status as an interviewer,
you need to add to what we've already covered. And add a new layer
of listening.

Learn to ask *open questions*.

'Don't you hate sneakers?' is a closed question. It allows only
two answers: yes, or no.

'What kind of shoes do you like?' is an open question. It allows
a vast range of answers.

'Do you listen to *The Last Word?*' is a closed question.

'What radio programmes do you listen to?' is an open question.
A good rule of thumb is that questions beginning 'Do you' tend
to be closed, whereas questions beginning 'How' tend to be open.

Learn to ask *appreciative questions*:

'How did you cut through the bureaucracy?'

'How did you keep your courage up?'

Learn to ask *directive questions*:

'Talk to me about...?'

'Go on?'

Learn to ask s*ilent questions*. Raised eyebrows can keep get
someone talking. As can a smile.

While you're asking questions, you should be moving into
a new level of listening. It's called Listening to Differentiate and
Remember.

Differentiation is the first task. Because we're all drowning in
information, we cluster and dismiss a lot of what we hear on any
given day. Some clusters are obvious. There's the Monday morning
cluster, when people talk about their weekend, their golf game or
their trip to Budapest. Been there, done that. Heard it before. We
listen with half our minds and make appreciative murmurings. Half
an hour later, we'd be hard put to recall anything the other person
has said. Because we've clustered and discarded it as 'Stuff I've
heard before.' It may not be identical to what we've heard before,
but there's a sameness to it.

Listening to differentiate means actively seeking to capture
what is *different* about this speaker and their topic. That means
refusing to accept the obvious.

'Budapest is such a lovely old European city.'

'How do you mean, exactly?'

Similarly, if they talk about 'a lovely atmosphere' in a restaurant,
push them to describe the elements that add up to that atmosphere.
Be determined, as you listen, to learn different aspects of each topic
from the ones with which you're already familiar.

Listen and question as if you were going to write a feature about
the topic directly afterwards or send an e-mail to a friend about it.

Listen and observe as if you were going to have to mimic the speaker to an audience – you'll be surprised at what you notice about them.

Listen as though you had to report the content to someone a few hours later. This forces you to concentrate.

One of the inevitable payoffs to Listening to Differentiate and Remember is that people become more interesting. Geothe said that if we treat people as they are, they'll never amount to much, but if we treat them as they might be, their potential is endless. Whenever you treat someone as if they were the celeb you've always wanted to meet, the person you know you will find fascinating, it stimulates them to be more illustrative and engaging than they ever planned to be.

Paradoxically, they also find *you* more interesting. You may think you're interesting because you're a raconteur, a good presenter, a joke-teller. Other people will find you interesting because you give them the wonderful free gift of your attention. We all go through life with an invisible tattoo on our foreheads, reading 'Please find me interesting.' Good listening meets that essential human need to be found worth listening to.

If you've stayed with me thus far but are saying to yourself, 'I don't talk that much at the best of times. I'm painfully shy,' then you should reread this chapter. Because the ability to interview other people is the ultimate cure for shyness. Instead of trying to make small talk, or, worse still, having to talk about yourself, once you get into the habit of interviewing those around you, you are always in a safe place. Because you always have a bunch of friends ready to go to work for you and take the attention (including your own attention) off yourself. Rudyard Kipling's little bit of doggerel sums it up neatly:

> *I keep six honest serving-men*
> *(They taught me all I knew);*
> *Their names are What and Why and When*
> *And How and Where and Who.*

I send them over land and sea,
I send them east and west;
But after they have worked for me,
I give them all a rest.

TIP

The day you hear yourself saying, 'I always tell people that...' or 'I like to say...' is the day you're overdue for remedial work on your listening. Bad enough to be an appreciative audience for yourself. It's much worse to be an appreciative audience for your own repetitions.

TIP

The day someone says to you, 'I don't know why I'm telling you this,' or, 'I've never told anybody this before,' pat yourself on the back. It means they find you a good listener.

Wisdom is what you get from a lifetime of listening
when you'd rather have been talking.

Aristotle

3

MEETING, GREETING AND WHAT'S YOUR NAME AGAIN?

Why is cold-calling the task dreaded by sales reps?

Why do people say they're 'bad at names'?

Why do some people leave a bad first impression?

They're all aspects of the same problem. The meet-and-greet problem. The getting-to-know-you problem. And you know something? It's been a problem for as long as humans have been around. Our very method of greeting a stranger – offering our right hand to shake theirs – started off as a way of showing that the hand was empty. It didn't hold a shiv or a sword: you're safe with me, Guv.

Similarly, the curtseys which used to be part of a deb's skillbase were a way of indicating subservience. Like an animal lying down and showing its weak parts, the curtsy or bow was a way of saying, 'You're more important than I am, and I know it.'

Most animals, at first meeting, quickly work out which of them is strongest. Humans are no different. Throughout history, the point of greeting has been used by one side or the other to establish the pecking order in the relationship.

Arguably the most extreme example happened in a little village in the middle of the northern part of Italy in 1077, when the Holy Roman Emperor, Henry IV, came to see Pope Gregory VII, with whom he'd had a bit of a tiff, leading to his excommunication. Excommunication, at the time, was the ultimate punishment doled out by the Church, and Henry wanted out from under its strictures.

When he arrived at Canossa, the Emperor was not admitted to

the fortress where the Pope was staying. For three days, he had to walk around in the snow outside, fasting and wearing only a hairshirt to indicate his penitence. Eventually, the Pope let him in and he knelt down in ritual apology. As greetings go, this one was fairly severe, although rumours have always done the rounds that Henry didn't really stand, stamping his bare feet in the snow outside the walls for all that time, but snuck down to the local village for a pint now and again.

While we don't, in the twenty-first century, do a Canossa on people (although most of us would love to get the chance) we frequently see the hostile greeting represented by the two-finger sign. The two-finger sign is reputed to have started back in the Hundred Years' War (14th–15th century). According to legend it was common practice for the French to cut off the first two fingers of the right hand of any captured English archer. This saved the cost of keeping them as prisoners or the hassle of burying them. They could just be maimed and released, as without their bow-fingers they were essentially useless. Rendering an English longbow archer useless was the equivalent of – today – shooting down an Apache helicopter; they were the most feared part of the English war machine.

The story goes that at the start of the Battle of Agincourt in 1415 the English archers all held up the two fingers on their right hands to the French army to show they still had them, could still use them, and, with them, were about to rain terror and vengeance on the French.

Today, our way of meeting and greeting usually involves looking at the other person, perhaps smiling at them, and shaking hands with them.

Usually. Not always.

One exception is the rude person who's so busy with the task they're on that they can extend a hand but can't find the time to look away from their computer or calculator. Another is the rude person who glances at a newcomer at the point of handshake, but whose gaze immediately defocuses as they look past that newcomer to see if anybody more interesting or important is coming along.

Neither behaviour is acceptable. No matter what you're doing, when introduced to someone new, you should put it down, turn around and devote your entire attention to the new person. Just imagine for a moment that this new person was going to turn out to be the most important person you ever met: the love of your life, the boss of your life, the friend you'd die for. If, years after your first meeting, that person commented that you had been surly and unpleasant on that day, you'd feel rotten about it. So make the assumption, every time you meet someone new, that they're going to bring something positive and important to your life and greet them accordingly.

That means a warm handshake. It *doesn't* mean offering a limp hand, hanging from the end of a wrist like a dead fish. Nor does it mean offering the stiffened fingers, rather than the whole hand, like a visiting member of the British royal family. The best handshake is where the skin at the base between thumb and forefinger of one handshaker meets the same point in the other hand. Firm grip. Firm shake. Disengage. (If you're not sure, ask someone to shake hands with you and get their frank judgement of how well you do it. Because a bad handshake contributes to a dire first impression.)

Men shouldn't do the knuckle-crunch shake that sets out to intimidate the other person: *See, I could break every bone in your body, I'm so macho.* Politicians have a particular handshake which involves warmly grasping the elbow of the shaken hand with the politician's left hand. It maximises contact in a decent way and that's all there is to say about it.

The meet-and-greet stage of relationships is the point at which we measure the other person up. If we're shy or unsure of ourselves, we measure ourselves at the same time: *I'm not dressed right. I missed that person's name. That other person looks much more cool and casual than I do. I bet they know I'm nervous.* We create a vicious circle, a feedback loop of self-destructive negativity.

The way to interrupt that feedback loop is to concentrate on the other person. On making that other person feel good. Not on making *yourself* feel good. A warm handshake is a start. Smiling at the other person is a good next step. Getting their name is the capstone.

No, don't say, 'But I'm bad with names.'

That lets you off the hook. And it's a hook you shouldn't want to get off. Our names are vitally important to us. They're among the earliest words we recognise, because people say them so frequently to us when we're small. They're among the last words we respond to in life – in any Intensive Care Unit, nurses can be heard, loudly calling out first names to comatose patients in the hope of rousing them. The same nurses will use first names with patients coming out of general anaesthetics, too, because it creates in the foozled patient a sense of being known and cared for.

The reason we lose names is that we don't catch them in the first place. When we're introduced, we're often so focused on ourselves, we don't quite hear the new name.

RULE #1: MAKE SURE YOU HEAR EACH NEW NAME

If the ambient noise means you don't quite hear it, stop and ask: 'Sorry – is that *Mar*ie or Mar*ie*?' Or: 'I didn't quite hear – are you Gerald or Gerard?'

RULE #2: USE THE NAME IMMEDIATELY

'Marie, do you know Gerard?'

'Gerard, d'you work with Marie or are you in a different plant altogether?'

RULE #3: QUOTE PEOPLE BY NAME

'Gerard, John was just saying before you joined us that…'

RULE #4: EMBED NAMES IN YOUR TECHNOLOGY

Getting telephone numbers is a great way to do this. Find a way to make a note about something that makes the person unique.

RULE #5: REVISE BEFORE NEXT ENCOUNTER

If you know you're going to meet Gerard or Marie again, take a few minutes as you drive to the location to recall something they talked about. Even if you don't mention it, it will help you to push their name and reality into your long-term memory bank.

You're now competent to capture names, a central plank in the building of relationships. Your competence will also mean you give a first impression of confidence and warmth to the people for whose introduction to each other you take responsibility.

Crept that one up on you, didn't I?

Introducing one person to another used to be taught in etiquette schools. Before they were presented to the Queen in court, young English girls were sent off to finishing schools in Switzerland to learn how to get in and out of cars without showing the tops of their silk stockings. Ah, well...

The pre-debs also learned how to introduce one person to another according to the rigid protocols of the upper classes at the time. Some of those protocols have come down to us, in watered-down form. Because they work.

YOU INTRODUCE AN UNELECTED PERSON TO AN ELECTED OFFICIAL
'Senator Norris, allow me to introduce you to my publisher, Jo O'Donoghue.'

YOU INTRODUCE A COLLEAGUE TO A CLIENT OR CUSTOMER
'Alan, this is Hilary Kenny. Our Media and Communications Unit is headed by Hilary.'

YOU INTRODUCE A JUNIOR EXECUTIVE TO A SENIOR ONE
'Dermot, I don't think you've met Gavan Flinter? Gavan's one of the best of our new crop of trainers.'

YOU INTRODUCE A JUNIOR MILITARY OFFICER TO A SENIOR OFFICER
'General, may I introduce Lieutenant Jones?'

The junior-to-senior applies if you're introducing churchmen or individuals within any hierarchy to each other.

You'll see, in several of the introductory phrases given, that I've repeated the new person's first name, because it improves the chances of the other individual remembering and using it.

Where you're introducing friends to each other, there's a strong case for adding some information which indicates the way you feel about them.

'John, you have to meet Suzi Carroll. Suzi's been a close friend of ours for fifteen years. She saves my life when I lose things like driver's licences. She's one of those people who knows how every system works and how to rescue morons like me...'

If you get a blank when you should be introducing people to each other, say so. But make sure it's a double-blank:

'I'm having a panic attack – you both know I know you, but both your names have gone phht. Introduce yourselves while I get us all a drink.'

In any social gathering, anticipate that this may happen to some-one else and so, the moment you're pointed at a new person, extend your hand and give your name. It saves everybody trouble.

If you're ever introduced wrongly, don't humiliate the person who made the mistake. For several years, I was introduced as 'Terry Keane' because that was the name of the then Taoiseach's companion, and gossip about her kept her at the top of public consciousness. It was important, in that situation, to prevent the person who had wrongly introduced me from feeling like a complete fool, so I developed a way of fixing the surname while moving into conversation immediately.

Where possible, start the conversation by pointing to something Person A does which would be of interest to Person B. All the better if the suggestion carries the implication that you've already talked to the other person about the individual you're now addressing:

'Fergus, I told Vincent you'd tell him your story about the politician and the nuns – it's one of the funniest things I've ever heard.'

If you're a man being introduced to a Muslim woman, do not offer to shake hands – she is likely to say, 'No thank you,' which can be unnerving.

Of course, every now and then, people finds themselves in a crowded situation where nobody takes charge of introductions. In that situation, you have a choice. You can stand on the sidelines looking hunted, your inner voice saying, 'I hate this, I really hate it,' or you can spot someone else who is on their own and decide, 'I'm going to introduce myself and find out something interesting about that person.'

It's the old rule of *Do as you would be done by.* If you were on your own in a crowded room, wouldn't *you* like a friendly human to join you, end your isolation and find you interesting?

The first task is to physically get to them. Don't dither. The University of California surveyed 10,000 people who had made an expensive service purchase to find out the key factors influencing them to say yes to the seller. More than half of them (55 per cent) mentioned that the person from whom they bought moved in a way that looked confident and comfortable.

So, whether it's at a conference, a party or a reception, when you've decided to cross the room to talk to someone on the other side, it helps if you give an impression of ease and self-assurance.

HERE'S HOW

- Walk as you'd walk to meet your best friend if he/she had unexpectedly turned up.
- Don't apologise your way across the room. Be purposeful and sure as you ask people to let you pass.
- Keep your head up.
- Don't saunter with your hands in your pockets.
- Don't weigh yourself down with impedimenta particularly impedimenta awkward to carry. Ditch them in the cloakroom or leave them in the boot of your car. One of the problems about items like phones, pens and keys is that we tend to hold them in our right hand – the hand we're going to extend when we introduce ourselves. Inevitably, this results at best in an awkward transition, right at the point of introduction, when we should be focusing on the other person, or, at worst, in dropped phones or keys. Women should never carry handbags big enough to contain a small SUV.

- Don't do body-protective gestures like crossing your left hand over to clutch your right arm. Coming into a crowded room 99 per cent of women put one hand across their bodies, ostensibly to play with the strap of a shoulder bag. It's an unconscious don't-hit-me defensive move. The woman doesn't know she's doing it but it makes her look less potent. Learn to enter a room with one hand – your left – on or carrying your handbag, the other hanging. And learn to look as if arriving in this room was the best thing that's happened to you all day. It's called, in psychology-speak, 'Behaving as if…' Behaving as if you're confident convinces other people you're confident and this starts a feedback loop that convinces *you* you're confident.
- Learn to walk confidently with your hands by your sides.
- (Hint: actors are taught to imagine they're carrying heavy glass balls – one in each hand.)
- Keep your head up, and if you meet someone's eyes while crossing the room, do a visual 'Howya'. It's no more than slightly raised eyebrows, but it says 'I see you and acknowledge you,' and allows you, later, to join that person and introduce yourself because you half-know the person already.
- Don't look at the person you're going to meet all the time as you cross the room – it would make them feel too much like a target being homed in on.

Be clear about all this sequence. Nodding as you read it and thinking 'That makes sense' is only the first step. Habits don't happen because we think they'd be good to have. Habits happen because we rehearse and do. Rehearse (in advance) and do (at the encounter) each of these actions and within a matter of weeks, they will have become reflexes. You won't have to think about them. Remember when you learned to drive a car and you had to learn to declutch and accelerate and – in the beginning – the car hiccupped and stalled because, even though you knew, intellectually, the sequence you needed to go through, that sequence had not become a reflex? If you're an experienced driver, you know that, these days, you don't even think about the clutch or the accelerator. The right actions have become reflexes. Part of your muscle memory.

That's how confident communication works. Rehearse and do until it becomes a reflex, then you can move on to the next communication skill.

When you reach the person you've walked across to, you can tell them you know who they are and wanted to ask them about some area of their operation. You can tell them that since neither of you hasn't been dragged into a group, you thought the two of you should start your own group. At a conference, you can tell them you missed some of the morning's items and ask what did so-and-so cover? Or you can simply give your name and ask their name.

Once you're introduced, you're ready to stand and talk. Stand in a way that puts the other person at their ease. Don't stand too close to them. Anthropologist Edward T. Hall has mapped out four distances which typify the level of comfort we have with different kinds of people.

Inside eighteen inches is what he calls 'Intimate Space'. That's where we welcome children, spouses – people we're very close to. Outside that is an area called 'Personal Space'. We allow relatives and close friends into our personal space.

At receptions and formal business encounters, on the other hand, we keep what Hall calls a 'Social Distance'. Social distance requires that we stand perhaps four feet away from the individual we're talking to. Although crowded rooms sometimes force us into tighter proximity, that's the kind of distance appropriate when we know someone, but don't know them well enough to move into personal space with them.

The last kind of space, Public Space, is for strangers. Especially strangers who are going to *stay* strangers. In situations like buses, trains and lifts, where we're in close proximity to strangers who are going to stay strangers, we depersonalise them by looking past them, looking at the floor or at advertising signs.

So: don't stand too close to someone you don't know well, and don't touch a new acquaintance in order to emphasise a point.

Stand at an angle, rather than shoulder to shoulder, face to face. Standing at an angle will ensure neither of you feels trapped and will allow another person to join you without feeling they're interrupting either an intimate encounter or a pitched battle.

Eye contact is important, but not in the way it's usually sold. When we have a real interest in another person, we do tend to look at them. But we don't keep our eyes glued to the other person in what the Americans call 'four-eye contact'. Don't start with the mechanics. Start with the emotional reality. If you decide to be interested in someone, then your eye contact will be just fine.

When you're really paying attention to someone, you look it. You *don't*:

- Allow one foot to tap or jiggle.
- Fiddle with small change in your pocket or with the clicker on the end of a pen.
- Permit electronic interruption by mobile phone.
- Go 'Am-m-m,' meaning 'Don't take so long to get to the point, you boring person.'

H. L. Mencken said that altruism is grounded upon the fact that it's uncomfortable to be surrounded by unhappy people. That's one good reason for learning names, registering the importance of individuals and creating contact: it creates a much easier atmosphere for everybody.

4

MAKING A PRESENTATION

Your mouth is dry but your palms are damp.

You woke up three times last night with an overwhelming sense of dread.

You have to give a presentation.

And if you think you're alone with your terror, you couldn't be more wrong. Fear of public speaking comes at the top of the list of personal fears, way ahead of the dentist, despite the fact that so many people have to do it regularly as part of their job.

It's a transport problem, that fear. People who'd make you fall off a bar stool with laughter can't transport their wit into the more pressured context of a boardroom. Friends whose e-mails are stuffed with interesting information get an attack of the waffles when they have to make a best-man speech. Colleagues who are brief and to the point on the phone go AWOL when speaking at a seminar.

Good communicators often become bad presenters because they listen to rotten advice. There's a lot of it about and it lives forever.

Take, for example, that mildewed old drivel that, when you stand up in front of an audience, you should:

- Tell them what you're going to tell them.
- Tell it to them.
- Tell them what you've told them.

If the man in your life arrived home tonight and told you what he was going to talk about for the night, then talked at you, and ended up by summarising what he'd told you, you'd hit him with a brick or get him medical help. Nobody does that in real life, one-to-one, yet someone, back in the middle of the last century, decided people should *always* do it when they stand up in front of an audience. In other words: once enough individuals are unfortunate to get together in an audience, they can be treated like passive morons. Not only is this outrageously disrespectful to every individual present, it's totally dated.

Television changed the way people listen. Not for the better. It shortened the international attention-span. But it also sharpened audiences' expectations. Audiences don't want big long context-setting introductions. They want speakers to be interesting, quickly.

Another piece of truly rotten advice is that oft-quoted bit of research alleging that 70 per cent of what an audience remembers after a presentation or a speech relates to the tone of the speaker's voice, their body language and their clothes.

What complete bullshit.

If 70 per cent of what the audience remembers is about voice, body language and clothes, it was only because they were subjected to one spectacularly lousy speech: they were so bored, they started to concentrate on the speaker's jacket, for God's sake. Put it another way. If you've been involved in an office Lotto syndicate and one of your colleagues arrives to tell you this week's ticket won and that you're a million Euro richer, the chances are kind of small that you'll make a mental note of the vocal tone, body language and wardrobe of the good-newsbearer.

A great speech or presentation never starts with getting voice lessons or rehearsing gestures in front of a mirror.

A great presentation starts with the audience. No, don't miss the importance of that.

A great presentation starts with the audience.

Most presenters start with themselves. With what they want to 'get across'. With the 'messages' they want to deliver.

Wrong place. Before you take pen or keyboard in hand, the first step is to sit down and work out who your audience is. Because a point that will make perfect sense to a thirty-two-year-old mother of two, who owns an SUV and a Labrador, will not make perfect sense to a sixty-six-year-old widower facing retirement. Write down a description of someone who represents the wider group you want to reach. Age. Gender. Location. Then two extra bits of information:

> *What they know – right now – about your topic.*
> *What they feel – right now – about your topic.*

The next step is crucial. Write down what you want them to know and feel about your topic after you've finished. If you want them to make a decision or do something differently after your presentation, write that down, too.

Once you know who you're talking to and what you want to achieve, it's relatively simple to assemble a talk that will deliver that outcome.

You need a 'gateway point'. A gateway point opens the door to the attention of your audience. Pick the single most interesting thing you want them to remember and put it at the top. Don't do lengthy introductions or settings-in-context. Cut to the chase. Grab them by the short and curlies.

Oh, and at this stage of your preparation, you shouldn't be sitting at a keyboard. Prepare for the spoken word *in* the spoken word. Walk around the room, making your points out loud. You'll often find that you don't like what you hear yourself saying. Contrariwise, you'll often *love* what you hear yourself saying. Write down what you like and keep talking until what you don't like fixes itself.

When you have worked out the key things you want remembered, work out the best sequence for them, so they link logically one to another. Failure to have that logic, those seamless links, is where you put yourself in danger of drying up: O God, I don't know what comes next. A good presentation has an organic shape to it. Like a tree. The speaker can illustrate a particular point (like the branch of a tree) but the central theme is always clear (like the trunk of the tree.)

It's only at this stage that a good presenter considers using technology. Sadly, thousands of bad presenters every day start to prepare by clicking on the PowerPoint icon on their computer. Presentation would be immeasurably improved, worldwide, if a virus ate that icon and the program it goes with. PowerPoint is that paradoxical thing: an improvement that makes things worse. Some American corporations are now banning its use, because they find it interferes with the ability of their younger employees to do critical sequential thinking. Bluntly, they get hooked on bullet-points.

Bullet-points are new to human communication. They don't have a magical success story, reaching back into pre-history, like stories and pictures do. Every race in every country at every time since humanity started has relied on stories as a way of understanding the world around them, because stories are interesting, understandable and memorable: the three key qualifications for good communication. We tell children fairy stories. We amuse pals with stories of disasters and gaffes. When it comes to public speaking, stories are an essential way to make the conceptual understandable.

For example, if a speaker says, 'Social outlets for otherwise anti-social tendencies are societally valuable,' we may be impressed, but we haven't gained *understanding.* If, on the other hand, the speaker puts the concept into a story, everybody understands the concept: 'My ten-year-old son plays soccer three times a week. That gives him a chance to work off all the energy that – if it was stored up inside him – might have him throwing stones or scribbling graffiti on the wall down the road.'

Pictures are important, too. If a speaker describes something so vividly that everybody in the audience gets a mental picture, it improves the chances that they will remember the picture and the point it makes, since synapses spark in their brain because of the effort to visualise.

Which brings us to the problems posed by PowerPoint. A PowerPoint picture is *not* worth a thousand words – because the audience gets it handed to them. They don't have to work to create it in their own heads, and so are less likely to remember it. Of course, that's assuming what goes up onscreen *is* a picture. Most of the time it's a series of bullet points or a huge chunk of text.

An even worse problem with PowerPoint is where it's used by speakers as a prompt for themselves. Prompts are necessary – and we'll come to the best method in a moment – but inflicting your reminders on an audience as if it served their needs, when it clearly doesn't, is counter-productive. The moment a PowerPoint presentation starts, the alpha waves in the brains of the audience flatten, as they decide, 'OK, this doesn't require any active involvement from me.' Passivity rules.

Cards are inarguably the best prompt method. Not a million tiny cards. A few sizeable cards. Carrying trigger words, not full sentences, written with a thick black felt-tip pen, twice the size of the speaker's normal handwriting, because the speaker will be under pressure and the words must leap off the cards at a glance.

Then it's rehearsal, to the point where the sequence and the illustrations are familiar, but not to the point where it's learned off by heart. (See Dos and Don'ts of Presenting.)

Still nervous? Good. You should be. (See Chapter 7.)

Business presentations are often made to colleagues. Colleagues are a difficult audience, because they not only know the subject, they often know the speaker. It's a challenge to stand up in front of people you work with on a daily basis. In fact, new research says that presenters dealing with groups they're familiar with communicate *worse* than if they were presenting to strangers.

'People are so used to talking with those with whom they already share a great deal of information, that when they have some-thing really new to share, they often present it in a way that assumes the person already knows it,' Boaz Keysar, a psychologist at the University of Chicago, commented when publishing the results of a study into communicating with colleagues and friends.`

Moral? Don't adopt a boring internal language, ostensibly understood by all of your colleagues, when making a presentation. Somerset Maugham said that the job of a writer was to make old things new and new things familiar.

It's also the job of a presenter.

THE DOS AND DON'TS OF PRESENTING

Do: Use cards. But not so many tiny cards you look
as if you're ready to deal out hands for a game of
Happy Families. The advantage of large cards is that
they are easier to handle than separate pages.

Do: Kill your mobile phone.

Do: Trust the audience. They're not out to get you. Every
audience has one shared, unspoken prayer:
'Please God, let us not have the knickers bored off us.'

Do: Look at them. Few openings are more offensive
than 'Ladies and Gentlemen' delivered with the
head down and the eyes scanning the script.

Do: Have water within reach. (Still, not sparkling.)

Do: Run short, rather than long. Leave them wanting more.

Do: Conduct a 'which hunt.' Go through any scripted notes you
have, searching for the word 'which.' Whenever you find
it, get rid of it. That will do two things. It'll divide one long
sentence into two. And it'll remove a word we use more in
the written than the spoken word. (Think about it. We rarely
say, 'The article which I am reading in *Image* magazine.')

Do: Suss out the venue in advance. It helps to know that
the podium has only slanted shelves which won't
hold a glass of water – you can ask the organisers
to put a small table beside it for that purpose.

Do: Prepare nuggets of added value for the Q&A.

Do: Be afraid – be *very* afraid – if you're wearing a radio
mike. Don't leave it on when you go to the loo. A CNN
reporter once did so while working at a conference opened
by the American president. Apart from the plumbing
noises, everybody at the conference also heard her diss her
sister-in-law in vividly pejorative terms. Because it was
a dullish conference, most of the networks represented
found this more interesting than the speeches, so her
views on her sister-in-law became nationally known.

Don't: Learn it off by heart. (Even if Churchill did.)
You'll develop a sing-song speech tone.

Don't: Hand your text (or hard copy of your PowerPoint
screens) out in advance. The audience can read
faster than you can speak, and will be tired of the
joke on page 11 before you've even reached it.

Don't: Use internal jargon or acronyms.

Don't: Imitate other speakers. Not their mannerisms, not their
quotes, not their gestures. Grow your own. Nor should
you *ever* take a text prepared for another speaker
and deliver it. In some large companies, it's standard
practice for the public affairs division to create a
presentation and distribute it throughout the organisation
to be delivered by heads of function in different plants,
sometimes in different countries. If the information is
that standard, and the imperative is for everybody in
the corporation to learn precisely the same data, send it
out in printed form. Requiring different personalities in
different cultures to parrot the same words diminishes
them and shows lack of respect for their audiences.

Don't: Take the graveyard shift. That's immediately
after lunch at a conference or seminar. People
go to sleep. Some of them even snore.

Don't: Wear something that's louder than you are.

Don't: Use a fully-typed script, paper-clipped together. That's not
public speaking. That's reading an essay aloud in company.

Don't: Take drugs. Or drink. Including tranquillisers, muscle
relaxants or beta-blockers. Dependence is easily created.

Don't: Tell jokes if you don't usually do so.

Don't: Talk through a distraction. When late-comers arrive,
welcome them and direct them to empty seats.
Otherwise, the audience can't hear you over their
anxiety that the newcomers won't get seated.

5

WRITING A SPEECH: FOR YOURSELF OR FOR SOMEONE ELSE

That speech is a flat failure, and the people are disappointed.

Abraham Lincoln to a colleague directly after he had delivered
the Gettysburg address, one of the shortest and most successful
speeches of all time. Lincoln was misled by the stunned post-
speech silence of the nine thousand people present.

Speeches and presentations have a lot in common. But they're not the
same. A man who makes presentations each week to his colleagues
and each month to his board will not regard that task as the same as
when he has to make a speech at his daughter's wedding.

It's different.

Another of the key differences between regular business presentations and formal speeches is that some speeches have to be
handed out to the audience or to the media, because they are used
to delineate policy or reaction to proposals. Another is that speeches
are frequently written, not by the person delivering the speech, but
by someone else.

Government ministers, for example, deliver speeches every
week that are written by civil servants. Sometimes, those ministers
might meet the writer in the departmental corridor and not have a
clue that this particular civil servant was the one who crafted the
words the minister uttered to a large audience the day before.

Most ministerial speeches are written in a people-free zone. The
writer knows the subject matter, but rarely knows the people who are
going to listen to the subject matter. More to the point, the writer
may not know the minister. The end result tends to be an amalgam

of earlier speeches – a paragraph lifted here and there – topped and tailed, traditionally, with a sentence or two in Irish, incorporating a written-word section on a new policy or government direction.

It's much the same in large companies, where someone in the communications or public affairs division crafts a draft for the CEO or the vice-president in charge of some area, without any direct contact with either of the two essential human elements: the person doing the speaking and the people doing the listening.

A version of the same thing happens with after-dinner and wedding speeches. The speaker, especially if they're nervous or inexperienced, gets the speech written by someone else. Too often, this assistance results in a yellow-pack oration which, even though it may be well delivered, does not connect with the people present in any real or memorable way.

Ministerial speeches often try to create an artificial connection with the audience by the insertion, early on, of a reference to the locality in which the speech is being delivered: 'So glad today to be in Ballysopfith, ten miles from the lovely townland of Boggins.'

A great speech, like a great presentation, starts with the audience. A phone call to the organisers of an event is a good start. That phone call can:

GIVE YOU THE TRADE/OCCUPATION/ PROFESSION OF THOSE PRESENT

Engineers, as an audience, are not like nurses, as an audience. The examples, illustrations and quotations which will make sense to nurses are not going to work for engineers.

GIVE YOU THE AVERAGE AGE, WHICH IN TURN DETERMINES THE LANGUAGE AND THE REFERENCES

Phrases like 'heads up,' 'early doors' and 'face time' will mystify an audience in their fifties and sixties. Phrases like 'listening to the wireless' or words like 'frock' are quaintly irrelevant to an audience in their twenties or thirties.

GIVE YOU THE GENDER

Men and women use contrasting versions of the English language. It has been estimated, for example, that 90 per cent of the similes and analogies men use come from sport or war. They talk about 'a level playing pitch' 'getting it over the line' and 'leading from the front'. They quote figures like rugby captain Kieran Fitzgerald: 'Where's your effing pride?'

Women, on the other hand, tend to draw their analogies from relationships, feelings and – despite the radically changed societal position of women over the past century – domesticity.

It's a mistake to underestimate the differences in style required for an all-female audience as opposed to those required by an all-male audience. Look at it this way. If a newspaper report says 'the candidate fainted,' nine out of ten readers will assume the candidate was female. Men collapse or pass out.

GIVE YOU LOCAL OR PERSONAL STORIES

This is of more than passing significance. A specific, informed reference to the current reality of an area creates a connection that a ritual mention will never create. Think of it this way. If a guest in your home says, 'What a lovely house,' it's a ritual. If, on the other hand, they say, 'This dining room suite is so simple and comfortable, it has to be Italian design,' it means they're actually paying attention to the place and thinking about the person – you – who made the design decisions.

Obviously, if you're writing a wedding speech for someone, you can't ring up the prospective guests, one by one, and have an exploratory chat with each of them. But you *can* talk to the man who's going to have to deliver the speech and get details from him about the oldest person who'll be present on the day, the most argumentative person, the sporting hero, the family with most members, the pals who have flown all the way from Melbourne...

Once you have a sense of who's going to hear the speech, you're immediately in a better position to write it. For example, many ministers believe that if they're not announcing a spend of

€3 million on something, they're not interesting. But, once you've talked to the people who'll be in the audience, you'll know that's not true. People have hopes and dreams and needs outside of local infrastructural spend, and the speech must reflect those dreams and needs.

Top of the list is the need to belong. For affiliation. Whether it's a family, a delinquent gang or a football team, people want to belong to something bigger than themselves, and speeches should acknowledge those important affiliations. Whereas a speech announcing a big spend may not connect with anybody, a speech which vividly shows how that spend will change the lives of people living in one small townland by cutting the time it takes them to visit their parents ten miles away will connect with that group.

Every speechwriter should know and be informed by Maslow's 'Hierarchy of Needs'. Abraham Maslow (1908–70) was a psychologist born in New York. Immersed in books by his immigrant parents who believed education was the way out of poverty, he was a solitary child, and, like most solitary children, an observer. He noticed something we all, in theory, 'know': that some human needs take precedence over others. If, let's say, you're starving, your hunger is going to be more important than your need for sex, since nobody ever died from lack of sex, but millions have died from lack of food.

Maslow eventually put human needs into a pyramid.

At the broad bottom of the pyramid are the physiological needs, the survival needs: food, water. Next up are the security needs: a roof over your head. Once a human being has achieved those, the next need is for love and belonging. At the top of the pyramid come what Maslow called the 'self-actualisation' needs. The need to do something worth doing. The need for self-respect delivered by a sense of contributing. The need to create, to innovate.

Bad political speeches play to the needs at the bottom of Maslow's pyramid. Great political speeches play to the needs at the top of it. They make us feel better because they help us eliminate our own prejudices, as did Jesse Jackson's famous 'They work every day' speech, in which he said:

> Most poor people are not lazy. They're not black. They're not brown. They're mostly white, and female and young. Most poor people are not on welfare.

I know they work. I'm a witness. They catch the early bus. They work every day.

They raise other people's children. They work every day.

They clean the streets. They work every day.

They change the beds you slept in in these hotels last night and can't get a union contract. They work every day.

They work in hospitals. I know they do. They wipe the bodies of those who are sick with fever and pain. They empty their bedpans. They clean out their commode. No job is beneath them, and yet when they get sick, they cannot lie in the bed they made up every day. America, that is not right. We are a better nation than that. We are a better nation than that...

The Jackson speech assumes the best of its listeners and speaks to their self-actualisation needs. It's also immediately understandable: short sentences, vivid pictures, story-telling. All of which may seem obvious. But it isn't.

RTE's *Week in Politics* programme with Sean O'Rourke, prior to the 2007 general election, brought over from America a man named Dr Frank Luntz to conduct three focus-group sessions with floating voters.

Dr Luntz brought with him gadgets which were distributed to each member of the focus group – literally, one for every member of the audience. The gadgets had a dial which could be turned to the left if the audience member found what they were listening to boring or negative and to the right if they found it interesting or agreed with it.

Sections of political speeches were then played on monitors in the focus-group studio. As each member of the audience reacted, their gadgets fed their reaction into a computer which produced two lines, one representing the views of people who had already indicated they approved of the government, the other representing people who didn't like the government.

No individual within the audience knew how any other member of the audience was reacting. So their responses to the speeches could not be polluted by peer pressure or by the desire to go along with a building consensus.

Yet the consensus built. Luntz's hand-held gadgets proved to be great examples of scientific measurement of understanding on-the-fly. What they revealed was not surprising to anybody who regularly writes speeches for other people: the minute any of the politicians in the film clips talked pictures, stories, examples, the lines indicating audience reaction went up.

By contrast, when the politicians talked conceptually or statistically, the lines sank. Why?

Because when we encounter conceptual language in a book or a newspaper, we can read, stop, consider the concept until we understand it and move on. There's no stopping in the spoken word. It comes at the listener in real time and must be *instantly* accessible.

An audience member who doesn't quite understand a point being made in abstract or conceptual language by the speaker cannot stop that speaker while the audience member illustrates the concept they've just been presented with. However – and this is the inevitable consequence of abstract or conceptual language by a speaker – the audience member probably will stop listening to the speaker while they try to work out what is meant. That's bad news for the speaker and the person who wrote their speech. Because, once the pattern of attention has been interrupted, it is unlikely to re-establish. Even if it does, the audience member will have missed whatever the speaker said during the time they were disengaged.

Speeches should never utilise abstract or conceptual language. Concepts can be made understandable by pictures, stories and examples. Arguably the best examples of simple (but not patronisingly simple) stories drawn from the real experience of the audience in order to allow them to come to terms with new and challenging concepts are the parables in the New Testament of the Bible. The story of three men handed the same sum of money by their master, two of whom buried it and one of whom invested it would have been interesting to the listeners at the time. It would have been understandable. It would have been memorable. The concept would have passed from one mind to another in a way which defines great communication. It must always be three things:

* Interesting
* Understandable
* Memorable

In the spoken word, the example allows us instantaneously to understand the abstract. However, the reverse does not happen. The abstract concept will *never,* in the spoken word, deliver immediate understanding of a proposition.

Now, let's be clear. This doesn't mean baby-talk illustrations. Dick and Jane illustrations. It means the simple, impelling illustrations Jesse Jackson used and Christ used, based on the experience of the people to whom they were talking.

Illustrations and anecdotes are vital in speeches, particularly after-dinner and wedding speeches. In that kind of oration, the speechwriter is looking for an anecdote about the bride or groom or individual in the audience that captures the essence of that person, sums them up, makes everybody who knows them say, 'That captured Gerard perfectly. Got him to the life. Couldn't you just *see* him in that situation?'

It's important to put in a caveat here. Some stories which capture an individual perfectly are not the kind of stories they'll welcome hearing in front of their mother at their wedding. Discretion and kindness should always take precedence over the desire for the easy laugh.

The desire to evoke an easy laugh also leads to repetition. This happens where the speechwriter knows a particular joke or anecdote has gone down very well in another context. Speechwriters should be wary of recycling proven lines and stories. Even the best stories pall with repetition. A few people in an audience may have heard the story last time out. But even if they haven't, the person delivering the speech may have difficulty refreshing the yarn so that it gives really good value to *this* new audience.

(One exception to this may have been Tony O'Reilly's tale of his return to rugby after he had become a rich executive, the punchline of which was someone yelling advice to the other team to 'Crease O'Reilly and crease his chauffeur while you're at it.' Male audiences steeped in sporting lore who had heard the story several times before nonetheless welcomed it, the way a crowd of pub singers welcome the chorus of a song they all know.)

One of the key preparation steps for anyone regularly writing writing speeches for someone else, be it a politician or a business executive, is to get to know your speaker.

An interesting example of this happened when I was training a writer to produce regular speeches for the CEO of her company. Realising that she hardly knew him, except as represented in the annual report of the company, she telephoned his PA and asked if she could attend a dinner at which he was speaking.

'I'm going to be writing for him, and I figure I should know what he looks like and sounds like and the way he thinks,' she told the PA.

'In that case, you need to know more than you'll gain by just seeing him on the platform,' the PA sensibly responded. 'Why don't you travel to the dinner and back from the dinner in his car and talk to him? Or perhaps I should say *listen* to him?'

It was a great idea. One-and-a-half hours to the venue, a half hour's speech at the venue, and one-and-a-half hours on the return journey gave the speechwriter an understanding of the man she could not otherwise have gained.

The following day, she noted down just some of what she had learned about a man who, up to then, had been no more to her than a name and a face:

- He was gentle with machinery and could persuade even temperamental technology to work for him.
- He hated cigarette smoke, and – even before smoking was banned in the workplace – would not allow colleagues to smoke in his office or boardroom.

* He could remember every bit of poetry he had learned at school and college. Because he loved language, he could also quote sections from the Bible and from films he liked.
* He loved gardening, was good at it, and had a particular affinity for the selection and propagation of trees.
* He hated informality in clothing to such an extent that he never took off his jacket or rolled up his sleeves. If you were at work, you should, he believed, be dressed for work, and you should, at every stage in your career, invest in the best clothing you could find.
* He was an intensely competitive bad golfer.
* His family was off-limits. It was clear from the number of calls he took and made on his mobile phone that he was close to his wife and children but he did not talk about them and went to endless lengths to protect them from public connection with him.
* Music was important to him. His car was equipped to play his iPod, which included traditional jazz going back to King Oliver but also a lot of Gregorian chant.
* Although he read slowly, and therefore got through only a few books a year, he always had a book with him. It was likely to be history, particularly social history.
* He had done oil painting in his youth, and a little sculpture, although this was not known and he did not want it to be known. He had a strong visual sense and an informed amateur preoccupation with architectural proportions.
* He had always owned big dogs and despised small dogs, particularly miniature poodles. Show him a miniature poodle trimmed like a hedge into a caricature of itself and he would become virulent.
* He was funny in the way he talked about his job and about people, but he was not a natural joke-teller or mimic. His humour lay in his capacity to view the obvious at a slight angle and convey that angled view so that other people found it funny. This was made even more effective

by the fact that the laughter took him by surprise.

As a result of one substantial encounter, his speechwriter had captured enough material to ensure that what she wrote for the man had a context and a flavour that were personal and authentic. In addition, because she had listened closely to the way he talked, she now knew which phrases would work well in his speech, what his sources of reference were, and how he behaved when he was working up to a major point. She was familiar with his gestures, the way he used a script and how he related to an audience.

That kind of research should always be done before you try to write for someone else. Once you know your man or woman, you can give them material that will sing.

Paradoxically, the same applies if you're writing a speech for yourself. Especially if you don't have to make speeches in the normal course of events, when you sit down to craft a wedding or after-dinner speech, you may start to write something which relies heavily on speeches you've seen other people give. Those speeches may have suited their speakers. They don't suit you.

- If you're not a joker, don't give yourself jokes to tell.
- If you're not a big reader, don't give yourself quotes from Euripides. Just pronouncing his name will pose a challenge to you.
- If you're handed a speech, or a section of a speech, the points from which you must make in your own oration, turn it into your own words before you incorporate it into your own script.

Other people can be very helpful when you're writing a speech. But the end result – if you're the speaker – shouldn't sound at any stage as if you are parroting someone else. Nor should any paragraph sound as if you hadn't written it.

Abraham Lincoln, one of the best orators who ever lived, used friends and family intelligently when he was preparing speeches. On one occasion, he asked a number of his cabinet colleagues to write paragraphs on particular issues for him.

One of them gave him this paragraph:

> I close. We are not we must not be aliens or enemies but fellow countrymen and brethren. Although passion has strained our bonds of affection too hardly they must not, I am sure they will not be broken. The mystic chords which proceeding from so many battle fields and so many patriot graves pass through all the hearts and all the hearths in this broad continent of ours will yet again harmonise in their ancient music when breathed upon by the guardian angel of the nation.

Lincoln liked what his colleague had crafted. He agreed with the sentiments expressed. But he also knew he had to work on it before he could *own* it, before he could deliver it in a way that would draw an emotional response from his audience. So he sat down and carefully rewrote the paragraph. This was how it appeared in the final version of the president's speech:

> I am loth to close. We are not enemies, but friends. We must not be enemies. Though passion may have strained, it must not break our bonds of affection. The mystic chords of memory, stretching from every battle-field, and patriot grave, to every living heart and hearthstone, all over this broad land, will yet swell the chorus of the Union, when again touched, as surely they will be, by the better angels of our nature.

Even in small phrases, the revised version reflects the man Lincoln was. The reference to guardian angels, with its implication of a *deus ex machina* power overhead, was changed to a more inclusive reference. It became a call to the intrinsic goodness of his audience when it changed to 'the better angels of our nature'.

The other step Lincoln made while writing a speech was to try it on friends and family. Not in writing. Never in writing. He would grab someone, pull them into a room with him, and ask them to listen.

'Sit down,' he would say. 'What I want is an audience. Nothing sounds the same when there isn't anybody to hear it and find fault with it.'

Even if the family member or staffer was too shy or too impressed to come up with criticisms, simply saying it aloud served Lincoln's purposes.

'Now I know how it's going to sound,' he would say, with great satisfaction.

This approach, however, should come with a health warning. People listening to a speech will frequently say, 'I'd put it differently,' or, 'Do you know what I'd say at that point?' The speechwriter should courteously note the point while always remembering that what someone else would say is not what the speaker would necessarily say. The speech must sound like the speaker does. It may be elevated in thought and purpose: speaking in public gives you the opportunity to put a new idea in someone's head. To make a group see the world in a different way. To give someone in your audience an insight that may change their life. To put on record (if it's a wedding speech) the unique character and special nature of the speaker's daughter.

But it must always ring true. True to the speaker's habits of mind, terms of reference, illustrations and language.

TEN TIPS FOR GETTING A WEDDING SPEECH RIGHT

1.   Take the pressure off yourself; you are not there to do stand-up comedy. You are there to talk to the bride and groom. As long as they are happy when you finish, your job is done. Their happiness will not be created by laughs and *doubles entendres*. It will be created by you reflecting the best of them and their relationship.

2.   Keep it short. You are likely to be one of four or five speakers. If each of them talks for five minutes that's nearly half an hour of guff. To people who are into their second bottle of wine and

desperate for a dance. No wedding speech has ever finished to cries of 'More.' (And, by the way, the Gettysburg address was less than 300 words long. Since we utter roughly 120 words a minute, you can figure how very short it was. In contrast to the speech given by the man who talked before Lincoln, who warbled on for hours and bored everybody.)

3.   Use humour (to make a point); if you 'open with a gag' you'll probably be praying for death before the end of the speech. Gags are high risk. If they work they're wonderful. If they don't they embarrass the audience and totally undermine the speaker. Follow the approach of most modern stand-ups; tell a story. Make it one that shows a facet of bride and groom and pick a funny one. That way, if no one laughs, you've still made a sensible point and no one is cringing.

4.   Cut all cliché. References to sheep. Calling them the 'happy couple'. Calling her the ball and chain. And all stories beginning 'When I first met.'

5.   Keep yourself offstage. No one cares about you. If you're the father of the bride, the husband's family and friends don't give a rat's ass about your theories and thoughts. If you're the best man, the bride's family probably don't know you from a hole in the ground and the groom's family may have had enough exposure to you to develop an intense dislike. The one factor that unifies the congregation is the new Mr and Mrs. Talk about them. Not you.

6.   Don't drink. Anything. Until afterwards. Then drink like two fish if you so choose.

7.   This is not a roast. Your objective is not to satirise, it is to praise. You come not to smartass Caesar, but to praise him. If you do decide to poke fun at anyone, make absolutely sure it is the same kind of joke the person would tell about themselves.

8.   When talking about the bride or the groom, try to see them as their new spouse does. Find the bits of them their other half loves and look for examples of those characteristics in action to quote to the congregation. Even if they put your teeth on edge.

9.   Talk it out loud before you give it. You should be used to saying
      it before you have to say it to a crowd.

10.   Mean it. Mean it on steroids. If you're the best man and you've
      been a best man before, that may have happened because
      you're part of a gang of lads who have been friends for years.
      Because you're the best talker, several of them ask you to be
      their best man. The real danger in that situation is that you do
      very well, for *you*. People compliment you. But – for the bride
      and groom – there's the faint aroma of performing seals. They
      get the sense that you do this regularly and there was nothing
      particularly special about their day. It doesn't matter whether
      you're the father of the bride or the best man, you should make
      a huge effort to deliver a speech that will make the day extra-
      special for the couple at the time and will, long after the day
      is history, contribute to the marvellous memories they keep of
      it. In that context, you should be setting out to be more than an
      amiable seal getting ready to launch the latest beachball from
      its nose.

6

WRITING FOR THE SPOKEN WORD

Even if what is required is a speech, a television script or a radio talk, when a writer sits down at a computer keyboard, what tends to emerge is written rather than spoken English. That's largely the result of education. We are trained to take the written word seriously. We write essays in college which accustom us to its structures, rhythms and formalities, so that even though the spoken word is used for as much as 80 per cent of our communication every day, the written word is the version of the language we take seriously.

In fact, the spoken word is important from the moment we're born. The written word comes later. The lexicon of the written word is richer and its products last longer – hence Oscar Wilde's expressed regret that he had poured out his genius at dinner and lunch tables, rather than making sure his every *bon mot* was committed to print.

The written word is the equivalent of a motorway: barred to bikes, invalid carriages, learner drivers, animals and pedestrians. It requires a bit of training and effort and adults do most of it. The spoken word, on the other hand, is for all of us.

That's not to say that the spoken word cannot provide challenges. Ava Gardner memorably observed of fellow film star Clark Gable that he was 'the sort of man who, if you said, "Hello, Clarke, how are you?" he'd be kinda stuck for an answer.'

Without being consciously aware of the difference between the spoken and written words, most of us instinctively make the necessary shifts. We speak in short sentences. We write in long sentences with subordinate clauses. We speak for immediate comprehension. We write for eventual comprehension. We speak with much more than words. We write with words alone and often too many of them.

Take a look at the following two paragraphs. They're in the written word. But they're a written-word version of a story you're familiar with. Trust me, you *are* familiar with this story. See if you can identify it.

> The circumstances surrounding the individual at the nub of the issue would suggest a precipitate loss of disposable income, although this precipitate loss is unexplained and is juxtaposed against radically different social conditions affecting near although not blood relatives. It is clear, however, that an element of envy over relative pulchritude may have been instrumental in the absence of the normal female affiliation one might have expected between the two siblings and their adoptive family member.
>
> The crucial intervention of a third party resulted from a social engagement involving the siblings but specifically excluding the central figure who was on her own as a consequence of their departure when visited by an individual claiming a spiritual relationship with her. This visitor then caused the manifestation and mutation of rodents and vegetables into means of transport into which she embarked having first undergone significant alteration of raiment, the latter involving items for the termination of her nether limbs of doubtful durability but immediate transparency.

That's the story of Cinderella with the written word inflicted on it. In the spoken word, the teller says, 'Once upon a time, there was a poor little orphan named Cinderella. She lived with her stepmother and her two ugly sisters. They hated her because she was so beautiful.'

Saying that 'an element of envy over relative pulchritude' may have caused the problem wouldn't cut it with a four-year-old. But moving into that kind of language, using what Macauley called the 'big, grey words of the lexicon' doesn't make it any better for anybody – of any age.

While not many people, asked to write down the story of Cinderella, would go quite as far into the written word as my example, the reality is that obscure writing is sometimes regarded as good writing. It often *looks* impressive. Indeed, most of us don't like the look of the spoken word when we see it on a computer screen or on paper.

Nicholas George, a one-time Director of News for the BBC, summed this problem up beautifully in a briefing document for his reporters. He told them:

> The best radio writing usually looks unbeautiful in print. We're not used to it. We speak one way and write another. What we would like you to do is write the way most people speak. Most people speak in short sentences or half-sentences. The language is usually uncomplicated. When you write a radio report, the language has to be uncomplicated. The language must be plain. Sentence structure should be simple. Simple subject, simple predicate. No compound sentences.

Bottom line: whether you're writing a speech or a radio script or anything else for the spoken word, write it in the spoken word and don't obsess over how oddly it looks in print.

Speechwriters may choose, if a copy of the speech has to be distributed to media or to the audience (always, please, *after* the speaker has actually delivered it), to rewrite sections of it so that it has longer sentences and looks more respectable. As long as there is no significant difference between the spoken word and the written word versions, that's acceptable. But, in preparing the version your speaker will actually use, prepare yourself and them for the fact that it won't look like a report.

It will, for example, have *short sentences.* Very short sentences. Sentences that may have no verb in them. Sentences beginning with 'And…' even if it would make the teacher who taught you English apoplectic. Short sentences are easier to read. Easier to hoover up off the page in one cognitive chunk which can be delivered *in toto* to the audience before the speaker goes back to the page for the next chunk. (It should be made clear, here, that this is not the ideal way to deliver a speech. However, many public figures find themselves delivering more speeches in any given week than they could hope to reduce to cards carrying trigger words, so whoever writes their speeches must make those speeches easy to read aloud.)

The rationale behind short sentences has been elaborated in what's called the Fog Index, which does complicated mathematics to illustrate that a sentence of fewer than eight words is easy to understand and that, as you double or treble the word count in any one sentence, the fog thickens around it, making it progressively more difficult to access its meaning at first hearing. When you've finished the first draft of something you intend to read aloud or have someone else read aloud, you can tell your computer to check for the length of sentences and cut the stalks down.

Another key characteristic of the spoken language is its use of *first-degree words.* A first degree word is one which instantly evokes a mental picture of what it means. 'Book,' 'boat' and 'cup' are examples of first-degree words.

Second-degree words almost have to be run through the first-degree filter before you know for sure what is being talked about. 'Volume,' for instance, can be used to describe a book, but it can also be a measure of quantity. It's a second-degree word. Similarly, 'vessel' or 'barque' are second-degree words for 'boat'. They're best used in the written word to avoid repetition, but in the spoken word, it's usually more helpful to the understanding of the audience if you stick with 'boat'.

The Americans call this the *KISS* rule: *Keep it Simple, Stupid.* They have a point.

This, for example, breaks the rule by being complex:

'The coming years are likely to see a significant decrease in national utilisation of fossil fuels.'

Apply the *KISS* rule and it becomes: 'Coal has had it.'

When writing a speech, for yourself or anybody else, write as people *actually* speak, not as they *should* speak. Don't put words in a script you wouldn't use to one other human being across a desk or a table or in a pub. Never set out to impress – just to inform.

One aspect of the *KISS* rule is making sure the words you give a speaker are words they can pronounce. Let's say your speaker is not adept with the sounds created by putting the tongue against the front teeth. So, instead of saying 'youth' they always say 'yout'. It's your job, as their speechwriter, to substitute 'young people' for 'youth' wherever it happens in the speech. And never overestimate the knowledge of your speaker. Put in a phrase like 'an old adage' and sure as shootin', your speaker will mispronounce 'adage' to rhyme with the Frenchified pronunciation of 'garage' so they say 'the old adahghe' when they should be saying 'addidge'.

The best way to avoid this is to listen to the speaker reading the speech and take out anything that they stumble over. Insist on its removal. I once had a speaker who couldn't pronounce 'ethnic'. Every time he came across it in the speech, he said 'enthic'. I wanted to take it out. He wouldn't let me. He was convinced he could learn it and would be more impressive if he did. I yielded. I shouldn't have.

On the day, as the keynote speaker at a prestigious conference, he got through all of the 'ethnics' fine, but ended the speech by announcing he was going to leave the audience with a quotation from 'Oscar Wilde's *The Ballad of Reading* Goal.' If you have to include a challenging word, type it phonetically in the version the speaker plans to use. *Not* in the version that's going to be handed out to the audience or to journalists.

Active verbs improve written and spoken communication alike. It's simply better to say: 'The Volunteers occupied the GPO,' than it is to say: 'The GPO was occupied by the Volunteers.'

State, then qualify, is a vital rule in the spoken word.

Consider this: 'There are exceptions to every rule, of course, and the metabolism of each individual is specific to them, which makes generalisations dodgy, but that said, it's fair to point out that a diet of chips and burgers makes people fat.'

By the time you have reached the last line of it, you've lost the will to live. And that's when it's in the written word in front of you. Say it as part of a speech or a script and your listeners will be totally confused by the time they get to the conclusion. You have provided them with too many distractions.

Do it the other way around: 'A diet of chips and burgers makes people fat. Now, there are exceptions…'

The initial statement establishes the issue. The modifications may be necessary in order that you be statistically accurate or for legal reasons, but they should come after the main statement, not before.

Mention people when it's natural is a rule of speechwriting that's easily forgotten, because we're so used, particularly when it comes to speeches, to a structure which puts thanks at the end, so that everybody from the plumber to the gravedigger receives gobs of gratitude in a wearying sequence. Much better to praise the plumber when you're telling the story of the burst pipe.

Postponement is impossible in the spoken word. Every time a speaker says, 'But I don't want to address that now,' or, 'More anon,' they create a distraction. This is made worse by leakage from the spoken word. The speaker who says, 'More on this following,' is as bad as the speaker who says, 'As I said above.' Above where?

The spoken word is *inclusive.* Inclusive means a lot more than using 'we' rather than 'I' or 'you' all the time. Franklin D. Roosevelt was once handed a speech in the middle of which was the line: 'We will strive to create an inclusive society.'

He opened his fountain pen and crossed out the line, substituting this one: 'We will build a society where nobody feels left out.'

Roosevelt's substitution turned the sentence into inclusive English. Use enough inclusive language in a speech, and the audience transforms itself. It becomes the embodiment of the ultimate inclusive sentence, Shakespeare's 'We few, we happy few, we band of brothers…'

In the spoken word, you *never reverse to the point.* In the written word, this often happens. Take the written-word version of 'Cinderella' in this chapter.

> The crucial intervention of a third party resulted from a social engage-
> ment involving the siblings but specifically excluding the central

figure who was on her own as a consequence of their departure when
visited by an individual claiming a spiritual relationship with her.

In the spoken word, we cut to the chase. The fairy godmother
appeared when poor Cinders was all on her own, crying because she
couldn't go to the ball the ugly sisters had gone to.

Although the spoken word has many virtues, it develops its
own brand of clichés. On radio, every day, you'll hear people make
announcements like this: 'Later in the programme, we'll be looking
at sex, lies and videotape. But first...'

'But first' is one of the maddeningly frequent clichés afflicting
people who make their living behind a microphone. Speechmakers
have their own clichés, starting with the lie about being delighted
to be here today. Every speechwriter, in addition to a *Dictionary
of Quotations* (to be sparingly used) should have a *Dictionary of
Clichés* on their desk.

In the spoken word, *repetition is valuable,* where it allows the
speaker to present a layered concept that increases in ferocity and
meaning with every repetition. The great master-orator, when it came
to the use of this device, was Churchill. On 4 June 1940, he made a
speech, one paragraph of which is filed under 'Half-remembered' in
many heads:

> We shall go on to the end, we shall fight in France, we shall fight
> on the seas and oceans, we shall fight with growing confidence and
> growing strength in the air, we shall defend our Island, whatever
> the cost may be, we shall fight on the beaches, we shall fight on the
> landing grounds, we shall fight in the fields and in the streets, we
> shall fight in the hills; we shall never surrender.

The repetition became like the beat of a war-drum – Churchill often
used repetition, and often in threes. He also used *sensational words*
– words that appeal to the senses – an essential of the spoken word.
Remember 'Blood, tears, toil and sweat'? Each one of them talked to
the *senses* of the audience. Anybody writing a speech should seek to

make the listeners' sense of smell, touch, taste and hearing activate their imaginations. Great art is always a dialogue, not a statement, and a speech can be great art when it evokes real emotional response from listeners by making their senses come alive.

One of the devices of the spoken word which should be economically used is the *rhetorical question.* The rhetorical question is a question that doesn't expect an answer. In Sean O'Casey's *Juno and the Paycock,* one of the characters, Captain Boyle, is given to rhetorical questions.

'What is the stars, Joxer?' he asks his drinking buddy, knowing he'll sound philosophical and get no answer. 'What is the stars?'

On rare occasions, the rhetorical question can be useful, as it was in Churchill's first speech as Prime Minister of Great Britain during the Second World War, when he asked rhetorical questions and answered them himself:

> You ask, what is our policy?
>
> I can say: It is to wage war, by sea, land and air, with all our might and with all the strength that God can give us; to wage war against a monstrous tyranny, never surpassed in the dark, lamentable catalogue of human crime. That is our policy.
>
> You ask, what is our aim?
>
> I can answer in one word: It is victory, victory at all costs, victory in spite of all terror, victory, however long and hard the road may be; for without victory, there is no survival.

Unfortunately, the rhetorical question is often the lazy speechwriter's method of moving from one idea to the next:

- So why does this matter?
- What is the next step?
- What is the problem?
- Where do we go from here?

The safest rule to apply to the rhetorical question is to limit its use to one outing and one outing only per speech.

Have the Courage of Your Contractions

In the written word, we are formal, opting for the full words rather than contractions. When we speaking, though, we litter our sentences with 'didn't' 'couldn't' and other contractions. If you're writing for speech, write the way speech writes itself on the air: with lots of contractions.

Make Your Sums Add Up

Every now and then, you'll hear a traffic manager or an environmentalist on radio, bemoaning the fact that only 1.2 people travel in each car commuting into our cities each morning. It's a truly ridiculous image – and, remember, humans *always* produce mental images of what interests them. What's point two of a person? Head and shoulders? Torso?

Figures should always be given in terms which make them understandable at first hearing. (And don't evoke pictures of sawn-off commuter chunks in cars.) Reduce them to the simplest form you can. Three in every ten, rather than thirty one percent. And don't put them in a list. If you give one set of figures, the audience will absorb them. Add a second and they stay with you. Add a third – and the earlier figures disappear out of their mental screen.

Do a Which Hunt

When you have your first draft complete, do a 'which' hunt. Tell your computer to find the word 'which' wherever it appears in the text. Then remove it. Its removal will make the speech more natural, not least because it commonly links two sentences which will be better, and briefer, on their own. But also because 'which' reeks of the written word.

REMOVE PADDING

Once the which hunt is complete, do padding removal. Here are some typical examples:

Padding	Brevity
Factual information	Facts
At the present time	Now
In the event of	If
A satisfactory consensus was reached	We agreed
Incapacitated in the performance of her duties because of the onset of viral influenza	Too sick to work because she had the flu

TIMING

The final technical task for the speechwriter is timing. On average, 120 words take a minute to say. So if you're writing a ten-minute speech, 1,200 words will do it. However, if you're writing a forty-minute speech, don't produce 4,800 words. Keep it below four thousand words. When speechwriting, *always underwrite*. Nobody has ever complained about someone ending a speech five minutes early, and conference organisers love the early finisher, because it allows the conference to get back on schedule, having been knocked off it by the majority of speakers who grossly over-run.

TEN TIPS FOR SPEECH LAYOUT

1.   *Don't type it in capital letters.*
     Capital letters are much more difficult to read than the usual mix of upper and lower case. We're used to the latter. Not used to the former.

2.   *Do use a serif typeface.*
     A serif typeface is one like Times New Roman (used here), where letters like M and N have little flat feet at the end of their uprights. A sans serif face is one like Ariel (used in the table above), where the letters don't have those feet. Serifs pull the eye forward and are easier for the speaker to read.

3. *Do use big type.*

Big type is fourteen or sixteen point. Unless your speaker is legally blind, he or she is not going to need anything larger than sixteen point. Indeed, if you go larger, so little appears on each page that a) the speech becomes disjointed and b) has so many pages that the audience think they're going to be stuck there until hell freezes over.

4. *Do use big margins and double gaps between paragraphs.*

This lets the speaker add hand-written ideas. It also means that when they glance down, they can see where they are and what's coming up next.

5. *Don't carry a sentence from one page to another.*

It's much easier for the person reading a speech if the sentence finishes on one page and a new idea begins on the next page. Making the transition from page to page while trying to finish a sentence throws most readers. Some speakers like to have the first three words that are going to appear on the next page put in the extreme right hand corner of the page they're reading. If that's what your speaker wants, give it to them.

6. *Don't put instructions to the speaker in the text.*

Under pressure, they may read them out.

7. *Don't staple the pages together.*

The speaker ought to be able to discard each page as it's read. In fact, speakers should always discard pages once they're done with them. Putting them at the back of the speech carries two dangers. The first is that the audience develops a hopeless conviction that this oration is going to go on forever. The second is that the speaker may slide the page into the wrong place and encounter a page they've already read.

8. *Do use thick paper.*

It's easier to hold and discard. Thin paper, on the other hand, allows the reader to be distracted by the shadow-images of upcoming points.

9. *Don't economise on paper.*

    Finish an idea on one page, even if it leaves a gap. The gap is a cue to the reader that they need to pause before attacking a new theme on the next page.

10. *Do paginate and order the pages.*

    Every now and then, you get a speaker who is so challenged (never mind why) that, if page 9 is duplicated, they will read the same page all over again. Even worse is the situation where the speaker hasn't had a chance to check the script beforehand and discovers, on the podium, that page 9 is missing or blank. Double-check that the pages are numbered and in the right order. In the main script and in the reserve copy.

7

COPING WITH NERVES

I'm convinced I deserve a place in the *Guinness Book of Records* as the person who has witnessed more panic attacks than anyone else. (I could be in there as a footnote as the person who's *experienced* more panic attacks than anyone else, too, but don't tell anybody.)

That's because I've spent thirty years preparing people to make speeches, deliver presentations and be interviewed on radio and television. Any one of which is more terrifying to the average person than going to the dentist.

I've had people faint. I've watched people go catatonic. I've seen people sweat more profusely than if they were running a marathon. I've seen people develop shakes in parts of their body you wouldn't think *could* shake.

I've also seen people produce 'remedies' for their condition ranging from tranquillisers to beta-blockers and from alcohol to Rescue Remedy. The latter tends to emerge from handbags. It's a liquid available over the counter in pharmacies, which claims to reduce anxiety. Since it has a tiny amount of alcohol in it, it may, in sufficient quantities, do precisely that, but when I asked one of our lecturers, a former pharmacist named Rory Fallon, to describe the efficacy of Rescue Remedy, he put it this way: 'It's roughly the equivalent of throwing a Solpadeine into Dublin Bay and hoping that what comes out of the tap will cure your headache.'

All chemical 'remedies' should be banned for public speakers. And for people appearing on TV and radio. The list of celebrities who have made a fool of themselves because of having take drink or drugs before an appearance is endless. It goes back to Brendan

Behan and R. D. Laing and comes up to date with Paula Abdul and the late Anna Nicole Smith.

Do you want to be famous for slurred speech, irrelevant giggles and a completely incoherent presentation?

No?

Then don't dope yourself before a public appearance. (Or any other crucial communications encounter.)

Doping starts when performers notice their own nervousness and make the assumption that it's a bad thing. It's not. It's a good thing. It's a *very* good thing.

The symptoms of nerves – wet hands, trembles, an urgent need to go to the loo, a desire to throw up – are all indicators of adrenalin pouring into your system. Adrenalin is the 'fight or flight' hormone. It's the hormone that helped our primeval ancestors to survive when they met an unexpected bear.

In one split second, while their brain worked out the options – run like hell or stab the bear in the gizzard with a sharpened stone – adrenalin pumped into their bloodstream to ensure that when they took to their heels, they could produce a fair turn of speed, or that when they stabbed the bear, they did it with enough force to put the animal seriously off balance.

Adrenalin is a wonderful hormone. In the past, asthmatics were given adrenalin injections to bring them out of really bad attacks. Not only did the wheezing stop in response to adrenalin, but the wheezer developed a confident high. The rush from the drug would convince the asthmatic that they were invincible. Nothing beyond them. Run a four-minute mile? Come on – three minutes would be no bother.

Adrenalin makes you think faster and more clearly. It gives an urgency and excitement to what you're saying that might otherwise be absent. (This is one of the reasons why, if TV or radio ever offer you a choice between taped and live, you should choose live, because the adrenalin flow is more pronounced.) It makes you slightly larger than life. All of which is good for a public speaker. All of which is *essential* for an actor. The day an actor is not nervous as she stands in the wings ready to go out and convince nine hundred people that she (coming from Coolock) is a Scottish noblewoman named Macbeth, is the day she's going to give a lousy performance.

Nerves are a necessary accompaniment of public speaking and persuasion. Let's say you're a nurse addressing a bunch of recent heart-attack survivors about smoking. You know that if they go back on the fags, they're likely to die. How you connect with them and communicate with them is a survival issue. A life-and-death issue. Of course, in that situation, you should be apprehensive.

Similarly, if you're a wannabe politician, making your pitch to the convention that will either select you to run as their candidate or reject you, the five minutes during which you stand and talk to them is a career maker or breaker. You should be nervous, because you need the added edge that adrenalin will give you.

Of course, you could do without the symptoms that adrenalin brings with it. Tough. Learn to cope with them. Start with not finding yourself guilty of being nervous. When the symptoms start, welcome them as what they are: the outward and (sometimes too) visible manifestations of the arrival of adrenalin in your bloodstream.

The bathroom is your best refuge when you have to cope with the symptoms of nerves. First of all, because those most severely affected may need to throw up. Only a minority get this nervous, but if you're one of them, it's important to realise that the episode is your body preparing itself for a challenge. Just as the hospital will ensure you have no food in your stomach before you face a general anaesthetic, so your own body ensures you have no food in your stomach before you face a major public appearance.

The restrooms are also useful if you feel faint. Sit down, get your head between your knees and – no, don't finish that old joke. That position, held for a minute or two, will improve the bloodflow to your head and prevent you fainting.

The less horrible symptoms of nerves still have to be coped with. Excessive sweating happens to some people when they are under stress, and this can be exacerbated by hot lights in a TV studio. My company always keeps jars of an unscented cream anti-perspirant (available only in the US) called Mitchum, which, applied over the face, prevents perspiration from coming through. It can also be useful for application to hands, because some job-seekers, knowing their paws are clammy and damp when they have to shake hands with the recruitment interviewer, get convinced that the interviewer will hate them from that first greeting.

Holding a script or cards when your hands are trembling from nerves is difficult. The pages will flap, establishing for the audience that you are shaking like the proverbial. BBC TV, in its early days, had a real problem in this regard. Long before AutoCue or SpeechQue, the BBC newsreaders had to hold the pages of their scripts up in order to have them in their eyeline. Many of them found that their hands shook. Someone in the BBC taught them a preventive measure, consisting of clenching both hands fiercely for a full minute. *Really* clenching the hands. Clenching them so hard that the nails on each finger left indentations on the palm of that hand.

The newsreaders were taught to do that during the sixty seconds prior to going on air, so that they held the clench during the thirty-second countdown, and just as the red light came on at the top of the big camera and the floor manager gave the 'On Air' hand signal, they would release their hands, pick up the script and start to read. Their hands could not shake in the aftermath of the clenching exercise.

The same tip works for voices. If you know your voice trembles when you stand up to speak, cover your throat with your hands in the lead up to your speech and clench your throat in a silent scream. Hold it for a minute before you start your speech, and when you do, your voice will be steady.

The two worst pieces of advice traditionally given to someone who is nervous about public appearances are these:

Relax!

To which the answer is, 'If I could, I'd already have done it.'

Take three deep breaths!

This stinker ignores the fact that most people, when they're nervous, hyperventilate.

People, when they're hyperventilating, don't use their

diaphragm, the big umbrella-shaped muscle below the lungs. When the diaphragm goes down, as it does when we breathe normally, it creates space, allowing the lungs to expand. That's why stage actors get trained in what's called 'intercostal diaphragmatic' breathing, so they have all the air supply they need for big dramatic speeches which must be heard by the people in the last row of the stalls.

Speechmakers who are nervous, in sharp contrast, don't create that space in their chest cavity. They just raise and lower their shoulders, filling only the top parts of their lungs with air, which, in turn, means that the lower sections of their lungs are filled with toxic waste: used-up air that hasn't been allowed to escape.

That used-up air cannot do the job fresh air can do – oxygenate the bloodstream – so it contributes to dizziness and to that roaring in the ears some speakers experience before a major engagement.

The first task is not to try to put more air in on top of the toxic waste that's poisoning your bloodstream, but to exhale to the fullest extent to get rid of it. As you're being introduced, breathe out until there's not a scrap of air left in your lungs. What replaces the toxic waste is wonderful fresh air that will dispel dizziness and allow you to think clearly.

One of the most predictable side effects of the arrival of adrenalin into the bloodstream is dry-mouth syndrome. Suddenly, your tongue feels like a brand new furry doormat and your lips are as dry as stale bread crusts. Sucking a hard sweet can help, but the obvious solution is to drink water. People going into radio studios always assume that the staff will ensure they have water and, nine times out of ten, they do. But on that one occasion when someone forgets, make sure, before you start to emote, to have a glass of water to hand. And use it.

Some speakers are convinced the audience will know how nervous they are if they see them imbibing water so they postpone it, ensuring the audience knows how nervous they are because their tongue is sticking to the roof of their mouth and they're making the distinctive clicking noises of dry mouth syndrome.

The fear of making a mistake is disproportionately large when you're nervous. Speakers in the grip of a panic attack are convinced that a) the mistake is the worst, most shameful, most humiliating anybody has ever made, and b) they cannot possibly recover from it.

Here's the reality. A fumbled word or forgotten name happens to every speaker, no matter how good, at some stage in their career. And recovery is a lot easier than you might think.

In my company, we discovered about recovery by accident. In the middle of a presentation skills course, more than twenty years ago, one of the participants dried up in front of the camera. She could not remember the next thing she was due to say. Waving her hands in front of her face, she wailed, 'Stop the camera, stop the camera.'

The cameraman, Gerard Kenny (now a senior consultant in our PR Division), is not a man who wastes effort so, when she flapped at him to stop the camera, he looked at her calmly and said, 'No.' Not rudely. Not sympathetically.

He just sounded kind of bored, as if it happened all the time. Which was the best thing he could have done because the woman, after a panicky minute, realised she had no alternative, pulled herself together and finished the talk.

When she – and we – saw the playback, she realised that Gerard had done her a great favour. If he'd stopped the tape and she'd had a chance to agonise over her 'failure,' she'd have had enormous difficulty resuming at a later point in the morning, just as a rider who falls off a horse and doesn't remount immediately is likely to develop a real fear of horseriding. She also realised that the entire episode lasted only a few seconds in reality, whereas when she was going through it, she was convinced it had gone on for ten minutes.

Mistakes happen. They are there to be coped with, just as you cope with latecomers (welcoming them and directing them towards empty seats so they don't distract the rest of the audience by mooching around pointlessly) or fire alarms.

Coping with nervousness tends to be inhibited by the conviction that nobody else is nervous. The reality is that every good public performer is nervous. And should be nervous. Just as every good public performer keeps, at the back of their mind, the memory of that one occasion when everything went wrong and they humiliated themselves in a way they hope nobody else will ever remember.

One last thing about nerves. Under pressure, when you panic, whether it's in the question and answer section of a conference or in a TV or radio studio, the first thing that will elude you is names. So make sure you have the names of all other participants and if necessary their titles, written on a card in front of you. This will obviate the possibility of your having to say, 'As my colleague on the right remarked...'

WORST CASE SCENARIO

The biggest fear public speakers have is of going blank. Of suddenly finding themselves in front of an audience with no clue what the next point is.

The solution? Very simple. Don't make the audience uncomfortable by pretending *not* to be lost. Announce it.

'Ladies and Gentlemen, I've completely lost my train of thought. Hang on a second till I work out where I'm supposed to be – Oh, yes. Now, the next thing I wanted to talk to you about is....'

The audience will think you got lost deliberately, in order to show how cool you are under pressure.

In the same way, if you forget a name, ask the audience for help: 'I feel like that singer – what's her name? The one who walked into the hairdresser's and shaved off all her own hair?'

Several people will laughingly tell you it was Britney Spears. And, because the people who have supplied her name have now begun a relationship with you, they're likely to be the ones who will ask you questions when it comes to the interactive bit later, thus removing that skin-crawling forty-five seconds while the panel wait for the first question, convincing themselves that the reason for its tardy arrival is because they were so boring in their speech.

8

JOB-SEEKING: STARTING WITH THE COVER LETTER

I know. You think a cover letter is such a minor matter, it couldn't deserve a chapter all to itself. When someone is going for a new job or a major shift in career, their attention should go to their CV, not to the cover letter.

Not so. Whether the cover letter goes by e-mail or on paper, it matters. It's the first encounter the HR manager or recruitment agency has with you. And it's too frequently the last. Because the cover letter's a stinker.

A stinker cover letter can take a number of forms. If it's on paper, the very paper it's on can be unsuitable. Three pages of lavender paper with a pastel drawing of a child smelling flowers in one corner are not the way to go. Nor is handwriting. Older readers may bristle at this. I bristle myself. Hell, a handwritten note is more personal, is it not? Plus, it allows the writer to demonstrate the Victorian elegance of their handwriting, does it not? Yes and yes. And no, neither matters any more. The reader of a cover letter wants no more than an indication that the sender knows about the company to which they're applying and is making an enthusiastic pitch to get a job there.

Cover letters should be on one page, should use the name you go by (even if your more formal first name is given in the accompanying CV), should make reference to any formal number or designation given to the job (in a big multinational, this matters) should carry your address and phone number and indicate that a CV is attached. Densely-typed cover letters running into several paragraphs warn the reader that the sender is either inexperienced or loves to warble on.

Much the same applies to your Curriculum Vitae. Keep it short. Except in the case of a medical specialist going for a job as a hospital consultant, few CVs should run longer than two pages. They should be crisp, to the point and carry no self-destruct viruses. Those viruses take the form of misspellings, grammatical errors and inattention to detail.

Recent UK research indicates that as many as 50 per cent of the CVs reaching recruitment agencies incorporate self-destruct viruses. They seem to crop up in the CVs of younger, rather than older, job applicants, perhaps because those younger applicants have come to over-rely on the spellchecker on their computer or on text language.

One of the worst of the self-destruct CV viruses is the yellow-pack virus (my coinage). The yellow-pack virus happens where a job-seeker develops a CV and decides that's it. No more work to be done. One size fits all. Never mind that the companies or organisations to which the CV goes differ from each other. It stays the same. Because it's been yellow-packed.

Making your CV immune to the yellow-pack virus requires that you always treat it as work-in-progress. Always ready for a tweaking which emphasises some of your strengths in response to the clear needs of an individual potential employer.

It's easy to be lazy and to have a generic CV on file, ready to be fired at any potential employer. Successful career-builders, on the other hand, make sure the CV which goes to the Buggins Babycake company stresses the skills and experience most relevant to babycake manufacture.

Getting a CV right also means avoiding over-reliance on the spellchecker. The only safe way to proof-read a CV is to print out a hard copy and read it aloud slowly and forensically, or (better still) hand it to a friend and ask them to nit-pick their way through it. A spellchecker is quite happy to pass either 'their' or 'there' or 'they're' as correct, because, in isolation, all of them *are* quite correct. They only go ropy when they're put in a sentence. Like this:

- They only go ropy when their put in a sentence.
- They only go ropy when there put in a sentence.

The spellchecker can't tell that there's anything wrong with either of those two sentences, but an HR director can. And when such an error is spotted, it announces a number of possibilities about the sender:

- They don't take care of the details.
- They don't respect the company to which they're applying.
- They're too easily satisfied.
- They're less than literate and could embarrass the company to which they're applying by incorporating that kind of error in official letters.
- They don't really want the job.

The most frequent errors are: misuse of the apostrophe, misspellings and inconsistencies. But some job applicants don't stop there. They move to the Hobbies or Pastimes section and fill in everything they've ever done outside of school since they were four, including listening to music (who cares?) going to the cinema (this is relevant how?) playing draughts or – arguably the most annoying of all – 'spending time with friends'.

The point about the Hobbies or Pastimes section is that it allows the job applicant to present aspects of themselves which may support their functioning in the job for which they're applying. If you're applying for a job with a sports gear supplier, for example, it may be of particular relevance that in your non-working time you play squash, climb mountains or go deep-sea diving. If, on the other hand, you're applying for a job with a company which sells those chairs which turn into beds at the pull of a lever, it's unlikely that your super-fitness will matter.

Britain's Recruitment and Employment Confederation recently found that one-in-five job applicants puts what they described as 'a significant lie' in their CVs to impress potential employers. That's unethical. But it also amounts, in many instances, to postponed self-harm. CVs stay around for a long time. They may sit in a file in the HR Department until the day you have an argument with your boss, at which point they go back over your file, and, discovering the lie, are in a position to take serious action.

A good CV does not require elaborate graphics, handcrafted paper or extraordinary length.

It must be clear, easy to follow and demonstrate, by the way it's written and presented, the sender's respect for the company to which it's being sent.

It can take one of a number of forms. The example overleaf (page 76) is what's called a resumé. It's a one-page summary of everything a potential employer might want to know about you, and it's the preferred form of CV in the United States.

More common in Ireland is the chronological CV, which lists educational and work experience.

Whichever type of CV is used must include the following:

- Name and personal details
- Educational achievements and qualifications
- Employment history
- Relevant interests and achievements
- Referees

How do you work out what's relevant in your interests and achievements? Put yourself in the shoes of your prospective employer and ask yourself if what you propose to include is of interest to them. They might, for instance, regard it as a major achievement if, having gone to university with a disability, you ended up heading a society or a club as well as getting your degree. Any position of responsibility which required you to be elected by your peers gives a prospective employer an insight into your character. When mentioning achievements, stress the skills you gained as a result of holding the position. These might include teamwork or motivational leadership strengths.

It's important, before you use someone's name as a referee,

Mary Rose McKenna
81 Mount Prospect Grove
Clontarf
Dublin 3
Ireland
Ph: +353 1 3333456
E-mail: mrosemckenna@irelandmail.ie

Objective: To obtain an entry-level position in business

Education: University of Dublin, Trinity College
                        Bachelor of Arts in Economics, June 2007
                        Relevant courses: Applied Economics, International
                        Economics

Experience:
Summer 2006:   Assistant in the Careers Unit, Carr Communications, Dublin
                        Dealt with customers on phone and in person
                        Developed a new evaluation form for the unit
                        Assisted on group courses
                        Filmed one-to-one courses

Summer 2005   Product Line Supervisor, Widget plc, Dublin
                        Met targets and deadlines
                        Worked within a team
                        Developed a new system of quality control

Summer 2004   Sales Assistant Tesco, Clare Hall, Dublin
                        Customer service
                        Trained in stock control and reordering

Skills: Computer-competent. Familiar with word processing (Word)
                        and spreadsheet (Excel) packages. Also competent with
                        PowerPoint. Fluent Polish

Activities: Chairperson, Debating Society. Led charity walk in Costwolds
                        that raised €40,000. Tennis club member.

References: Available on request

to get their permission. Then include their name, job title, address, email address and telephone number or numbers. *Inform* your referee about the job, what it entails, why you believe you'd be suitable for it. Mark their card on precisely what you want them to stress, should the prospective employer telephone them. You want more from a referee than their assurance that you haven't spent that much time in jail or crashed too many stolen cars. You want them to give day, date and example of specific situations where you shone. If necessary, having briefed a referee verbally, follow up by e-mailing or mailing them a package of data, including the job advertisement, job spec and your CV. Don't put the names of your referees on your CV unless requested to do so. And, in briefing your referees, make sure to ask them to let you know if they've been contacted.

Overleaf is Carr Communications' template for a chronological CV.

Finally, make sure the letter and CV are addressed to the right person, their name correctly spelled, with the right title at the right address.

If you're e-mailing the CV, read the instructions on the site to which you're sending your data. They may, for example, prefer you not to paste a CV created in Microsoft Word into your email, because, when it emerges on their system, it comes out as garbage. Or they may not like attachments.

It can be useful, when sending a CV and cover letter, to put them into one, rather than two, documents. When they get printed out in the recipient's office, this obviates the possibility that they might get separated fom each other.

Creating an Ascii/Plain Text resumé and cover letter and keeping them on file can be useful. They won't be as attractive as a fully-formatted version, but *will* be universally compatible. (To convert your file from MS Word (PC file): Open your document, go to Edit > Select All and change the font to Courier 12 pt; go to File > Page Setup and change the left and right margins to 1.5. Then go to File > Save As > Under 'Save as Type' select 'Text Only with Line Breaks.' Select 'Yes' at the box about making features compatible. Close and

NAME
Personal Details
Address
Phone
e-mail
(Driver's licence if required)

PROFILE
A proactive and enthusiastic psychology graduate with the ability to work as
part of a team or independently. I have extensive customer service experience,
through working in various frontline roles throughout college.

EDUCATION AND QUALIFICATIONS

2004 to date
National College of Ireland
        Graduate Diploma in Human Resource Management
        Exams this May

2001–2004
University College Dublin
        BA (Honours) Psychology: 1st class honours
        Major Subjects: Psychology, Philosophy

1995–2001
St Mary's School, Clontarf
        Leaving Certificate: six honours including English (B), Maths (C),
                                 French (B), Business Studies (C), Biology (B)
                                 Home Economics (A)

EMPLOYMENT HISTORY

May 2005 to date
Sales and Customer Service Agent
ABC Travel Agency
•   Delivered excellent customer service and travel advice to
         all clients on the telephone and face to face.
•   Consistently exceeded monthly sales and service targets.
•   Developed efficient organisational and administrative skills.
•   Awarded customer service agent of the month for quality service.

INTERESTS/ACHIEVEMENTS

•   First class honours degree in Psychology
•   Three months voluntary work in Thailand following tsunami
•   Set up hill walking club in college – now 100 members –
•   Organised... Member of... Won...
•   Keen interest in outdoor activities – hill-walking, cycling and running
•   I also enjoy reading and am a member of a local book club.
•   I am an aspiring cook, and enjoy cooking for my friends and going out for meals.

REFEREES

Available upon request

A profile gives a quick overview of you at the start. Keep the information concise and relevant.
Profiles can include
- Personal Profile – describe self, qualities, strengths
- Career Profile – track record & business skills
- Career Objective – you career goals in 20 words
- Key Skills Profile – summarises main skills relevant to job

Summary of education and professional examinations
Start with most recent qualifications
Include significant subjects studied relevant to job
- Dates
- University/college attended
- Degree
- Grades
- Major Subjects

Start with most recent job and work backwards
Give most space to most recent and relevant jobs
Include all relevant jobs – holiday, voluntary
Emphasise skills gained in each job
Use positive language – action verbs

Date from/to
Key Job Role
Name of Company
- Brief description of what you did
- Main duties of the role
- Skills developed in this role
- Achievements gained

You could choose to separate these out:

Interests
- include a broad range
- include individual and group interests
Achievements
- range of academic and personal achievements
- bullet point and be concise

reopen the file, which now has a text (.txt) extension, and tidy up any symbols that didn't convert properly, adding a series of dashes or asterisks to separate sections.)

Test whether the outcome emerges on other systems by sending it to yourself and a few friends.

Make sure, when you e-mail anything involved in your job search, that you use a personal email address, not one associated with your current employer.

When it comes to sending the CV and cover letter to a prospective employer, follow slavishly any instructions given. In the absence of such instructions, set your message format to plain text, not HTML. Enter the recipient's address. In the subject line, establish precisely the job for which you're applying and give your name. (*Never* put a general designation like 'Curriculum Vitae' which fails to distinguish you from hundreds of other applicants.)

Unless the target company has specifically requested no attachments, attach your Word resumé (.doc or .rtf file), so that, if they'd like to see a more pleasantly laid out version, they can.

A reality with which more and more job-seekers will have to contend in future is the Euro Pass CV. (See www.europass.ie.)

One final point about job-seeking on the Web. Make sure you have a good virus protection programme on your computer. Nothing damages your job prospects quite so vividly as delivering a computer virus to a potential employer.

9

FACING THE JOB INTERVIEW

Preparing people for upcoming job interviews or promotion interviews is one of those tasks that should, after a few years, get boring.

It never does.

Because, within the first few moments, the interviewee reveals so much about themselves.

They may:

* Reveal that they don't actually want this job at all. Their mother saw the ad and decided it would be perfect for them.
* Indicate that they will do anything short of murder to get it. (And maybe murder, too, if you tell them a touch of homicide would help.)
* Tell you that although they desperately want the job, they believe the process is a ready-up and the post has already been promised to someone else.

Of the three, the first is the most problematic. The person in front of you doesn't want the job for which they're going. Problem. The person in front of you is so in thrall to their mother that they don't have the courage to tell her, 'Back off, I don't want that job.' Instead, they cave in, allow her to pay for someone to train them, travel to the training company and – once they're there – engage in passive-aggressive time-wasting. It's not great career-planning.

The person who believes the job has already been given to someone else and that the entire sequence of job interviews has been set up to conceal that fact may be right. Or they may be wrong. It depends on their level of paranoia and their understanding of their potential employer.

But if there's the smallest chink of possibility, it's worth aiming for. Executives should always go into a job interview assuming the best of the person interviewing them and of the company or public body or civil service department to which they have applied. Anything else is counter-productive. The executive who leaves open a back door of excuses is the executive who does a weak and flat interview. Executives should always behave as if the process were open and above board. Suing comes later, if evidence presents itself that it *wasn't* open and above board.

Before the job interview, you'll have done research.

The research starts with the ad, if you've responded to a media ad, or with the notice, if you're applying for a change of position within your own organisation, and the post for which you have applied is drawn to your attention on a staff notice board or intranet site.

Read the ad carefully and work out the specific competences it requires of the successful applicant. If the ad states that a job specification is available on request, request it.

Reading it carefully will allow you to identify the competences you must prove in order to get the job. Because, even if it's not a competency-based interview (about which more later), what your interviewer panel will still be seeking is a series of competences. Not aspirations. Not characteristics. Not attitudes. Competences.

For an activity to become a competence, you must be able to do it consistently. It has to be a predictable part of your performance. You must be able to demonstrate how, in your career to date, that competence has been in play.

List the competences specified, or the ones you believe must be required in the job. They might include some of the following:

- Communication skills
- Strategic thinking

- Teamworking
- People management
- Capacity to manage complexity/competing priorities
- Understanding of the law
- Decision-making
- Business planning/financial management

Isolate each one and examine your career to date. Have you experience of, say, people management? What's your best example of that competence? Younger job applicants can be stumped by this, but a little lateral thinking may produce a project done at school or university where a group of disparate personalities had to be briefed, motivated and helped to deliver on an objective by a particular deadline without tearing one another's lungs.

Be clear, when you're seeking out the examples of your personal strengths, that you're not simply seeking out *experiences that you have had.* Aldous Huxley observed that the significance of experience is not what happens to us. It's what we *do* with what happens to us. Too many job applicants happily list off the experiences they've had without in any way demonstrating that those experiences have led to them possessing a new or enhanced capability, applicable to the job they're seeking.

In claiming to have a particular strength, you may first make a general statement: 'I have experience in crisis management.'

The interviewer will then need some specifics. So, in relation to a particular crisis, you will explain what resources you used to cope with it, what initiatives you took, how you approached the gathering of information, managed people, what results or outcomes emerged and how your contribution affected those outcomes.

But don't stop there. Indicate what you learned from the experience. What insights you gained. How you changed the system to take account of what emerged from that experience. Which of your skills was enhanced.

And then, if you can with reasonable subtlety, indicate where that strength and the extra skills-development resulting from its deployment would be useful to you in the job for which you are applying.

So instead of simply stating experiences you've had, you're now setting out to demonstrate:

* The experience
* The strength or competence on your
  part the experience demanded
* The learning which happened as a result of the experience
* The relevance of that learning to you
  in the job that's now on offer

The last is important, particularly to older job seekers. Older job seekers are sometimes in love with their past. They can talk at length and interestingly about what they did in previous posts. When they fail to relate that to the present, they turn themselves into an historical artefact, and create the 'that was then' mindset in their interviewer: 'That may have been fine back then, but how relevant is it to *this* job, *these days*?'

The interviewer may not vocalise what they're thinking. That doesn't matter. It's still the interviewee's task to constantly relate their past to their (possible) future with the company.

Preparation for job interviews starts with lining up the strengths you know you must prove you have in order to get the job, selecting the examples which deliver that proof, talking them out loud so you get comfortable and familiar with them, asking yourself the kind of questions the interviewer is likely to ask in order to give yourself practice at linking from the question you're asked to the evidence you must give.

If your CV reveals a discrepancy in your career, the interviewer will want to know about it. The problem is that you may not even want to think about why you left a particular job after only six months. If your last employer gave you a negative review and effectively paid you to go away, the experience may have been so upsetting that you gloss over it, even in your own mind. If you were bullied in a previous job and took legal action as a result, you might prefer not to relive the painful year or two it took to get the problem straightened out.

But you cannot afford to leave such a negative unaddressed in your preparation. Address it – not from your own point of view, but from the prospective employer's point of view. Put yourself in their shoes and ask yourself: 'If I was them, what would I be worried about when I spotted this bit in the curriculum vitae?'

Take, for example, rapid transit between jobs. Putting yourself in the interviewer's shoes will lead you to realise that they don't want to appoint someone who regards this position as a station on the route to something bigger and better. So they are likely to ask you a question along these lines: 'Where do you see yourself, five years from now?'

I recently sat on an interviewing panel for a PR company, where by far the best of the candidates, on paper and in personality, was asked that question.

'I would hope to have set up my own company at that point,' she cheerily told us. 'My ultimate ambition is to own and run an international public relations company.'

Great answer. It clarified everything. She didn't get the job because, when all the interviews were over and the panel was discussing her performance, the CEO of her prospective employer wouldn't even consider hiring her.

'What we want for this job is someone who wants to spend the rest of their career with us,' he stated. 'We need continuity, we need someone who thinks, all day, every day, about future possibilities, directions, markets. Instead of that, if we took this woman, she's be honing her skills on our time, making great contacts – on our time, building up relationships with our clients so she could take them with her when she got around to setting up her own company. I'd be out of my mind to consider her.'

You must never, *ever* lie in an interview. But it's your responsibility, in advance of any interview, to work out what, in your track record, might be viewed with suspicion by the interviewer, and how best to set their mind at ease about you as a potential employee.

The opening question in any job interview tends to be a soft and open one. 'Soft' in the sense that it doesn't require the interviewee to prove anything specific. 'Open' in the sense that it allows the interviewee to lay out whatever they would like to put on the table.

Many HR interviewers and panels devote the first five minutes of an interview to putting the interviewee at ease. They want to select the best job applicant, and they do not want to miss him or her by crating such a level of tension that a reasonably sensitive person who is, nonetheless, highly qualified, might fail to demonstrate that they *are* the best applicant. This may lead to an apparently loose and inconsequential initial discussion of why the applicant has applied for this particular post.

Even the most casual questions, like: 'So tell us why this job would attract you?' allow you to establish important facts about yourself.

One of those facts should be that you know about the company or the organisation. Each employer has a sense of their individuality. Hewlett-Packard sees itself as being quite different to Intel. Eli Lilly may be in the same business sector as Pfizer, but it regards itself as having quite a different history and corporate culture. The first moments of an interview should establish your understanding of the company and of the job. They should *not* let the HR Manager know that you basically want any job at this level in any company.

Now and again, particularly in a panel interview (see later in this chapter) one questioner may announce that they'd like to 'take you through your CV'. You should not plan the encounter based on this possibility. It happens less often than once in fifty interviews. Where it does happen, its objective is usually to help the panel, not all of whom can always be trusted to have carefully read each of the CVs supplied to them in advance of the interview. Even if they have, running through the CV is perceived as helping them distinguish between the various applicants.

Being 'taken through' a CV is not a guided tour through what is familiar to you. It is an opportunity for you to *explain the significance and relevance of each of the stages of your career or educational path.* You're not there to nod when the interviewer says 'And then you spent a year in India.' You're there to explain that the accountancy firm you were with at the time had a mobility programme designed to let young graduates gain overseas experience and widen their horizons, and that you picked India because the indications are that India will be crushingly competitive in certain markets in the immediate future. Explain what you gained and learned and make it relevant to the company considering you for employment.

While you must be ready to have your CV used as a device to take you through your work and academic history, it's important not to expect that it will be so used. Most interviewees kind of think their CV is what will get them the job. Not so. The CV will get you the interview. It's the interview or interviews that'll get you the job.

During the interview, regard the CV as the brochure that hooked them enough to get you to this point, but don't make any of these mistakes:

- Suggesting to the interviewer that they should refer to a particular page in the CV. They are not students, obediently following a lecturer's instructions to locate a page in a textbook, and are likely to find it discomfiting for *you* to be directing *them* in a situation where the protocol expects them to be in charge.
- Selling the CV, not yourself. Constant references to a CV are pointless. The employer is not offering your CV a job. It's you they want or don't want. So stow the 'As you can see in my CV' allusions.
- Failing to expand on something that's dealt with in the CV *because* it's dealt with in the CV. It's your responsibility to make the experiences briefly outlined in your resumé become real to the interviewer.

After the soft-and-fuzzy opening, the questioning is likely to get a little more pointed:

- How has your work experience prepared you for this position?
- What aspect of your career is most relevant to this position?

These more pointed questions allow you to start establishing and illustrating your competences. With enthusiasm. Management consultant David Maister maintains that good employers, no matter how technical their approach to the interview process, are always looking for 'the people with the shining eyes'.

The people with the shining eyes do not go into job interviews assuming that the interviewer is out to get them. They don't greet each incoming question as if it was a cluster-bomb. Instead, they welcome even the most negatively-phrased question as an opportunity to prove how good a choice they would be for the post. They understand that it isn't the interviewer's job to figure out the positive implications of any experience they present.

They know the interviewer is not a mind-reader and that they must supply him or her with the evidence they can later use to justify their selection of the candidate. It's all about evidence and proof, not assertion. There's no point in claiming to be a good team-worker if you don't go on to provide an instance of where you worked particularly well with a specific team.

The higher the level of the appointment, the more likely the interviewers are to ask competency-based questions. In the civil service, for example, if you're going for promotion, you will know in advance the competences you must prove, and you can expect to be asked detailed questions like this:

> Describe a specific point where your judgement (or capacity to manage competing priorities/deal with external bodies/communicate an unwelcome message) was tested.

However, even if the interviewer *doesn't* ask you that kind of question, you must provide that kind of answer. Never wait for the right question. It may never arrive. It's your task to provide the right answers. To put on the table the evidence proving that you have the capabilities the job demonstrably requires.

In addition to experience questions, interviewers may ask what are called 'scenario questions'. This is where the interviewer outlines a particular scenario and asks what you would do in that situation.

Scenario questions are valuable on a number of fronts. They're valuable to the interviewer, because they give the opportunity to observe:

a)   how the candidate listens
b)   how they analyse
c)   how they approach problem-solving

In addition, they move a candidate out of commentator mode. Some candidates are extremely impressive when they're commenting on issues like diversity or conflict as theoretical propositions, but may be markedly less impressive when presented with a hypothetical situation and asked precisely how they would respond in those circumstances.

When asked a scenario question, the first thing you must do is demonstrate that you have listened and understood what is being asked. If necessary, feed back what you have heard and ask if you've left anything out.

The next thing you must do is think. It sounds obvious, but many interviewees are convinced that if they don't fill the air with words during every moment of a job interview, in some way they are failing. An interviewer or interview panel wants to assess *what you would be like if you were appointed to the job.* If it's a senior appointment requiring judgement, the scenario question provides you with the opportunity to demonstrate judgement by considering all the implications of the question. There's no premium on speed of answer in that context. It's useful to refer to an experience akin to the scenario, which illustrates your competence.

Interviewers may also choose to ask you negative questions:

* You've spoken about your strengths.
  What's your greatest weakness?
* What was the biggest setback in your career? (Or
  the most difficult reporting relationship?)
* What's the worst mistake you've made?
* What was the most challenging crisis?

Inexperienced interviewees become extremely anxious when asked negatively-phrased questions. But a negative question gives a golden opportunity for a positive answer. Just make sure it isn't an obviously prepared answer. One of the most irritating responses to the 'What's your greatest weakness?' question is the simpering 'Well, I'm a perfectionist...' Perfectionism, of course, is not a weakness at all, so the answer is dishonest. Pick a weakness that does not immediately disqualify you, like fear of heights if you want to be a bricklayer on a skyscraper, and indicate how you have tackled that weakness and any improvements you've made.

I once interviewed a psychiatrist going for a consultancy post in a hospital, and – without malign intent – asked him about his key weakness. He took off like a vertical take-off aircraft and talked for thirteen uninterrupted minutes about his weakness, which was procrastination. He illustrated his weakness one hell of a lot better than he had illustrated any of his strengths, and at the end of the thirteen minutes had single-handedly proven himself unemployable, not just in this particular job, but in *any* job. He viewed the videotape of his performance not knowing whether to laugh or cry. When it was over, he knew that a mention of a tendency to postpone things is not the same as proving he had never in his life met a deadline and was completely unreliable.

You will, of course, be nervous. You should be. (See Chapter 7.) It may even happen that you lose your place in an answer. If you do, simply go back to the interviewer and say, 'I'm so sorry, I've lost my train of thought. What was it you asked me, again?'

Do the same thing if you've been asked a multi-faceted question and are not sure you've dealt with all the angles: 'I know your question had several issues to be addressed. Have I dealt with them all or did I miss one?'

PANEL INTERVIEWS

An interview conducted by a panel of questioners as opposed to one conducted by an individual questioner usually happens at higher levels, where the post is CEO, head of department or – in the case of healthcare interviews – consultant. They're more daunting, because the interviewee has the feeling that they're facing carbine, howitzer, Uzi, pistol and rocket-launcher simultaneously.

In fact, however, the task is the same. You have done your preparation and are determined to find opportunities to leave evidence of your relevant strengths with the panel.

Although the task is the same, the structure, inevitably, is different. Typically, the panel will have divided up the questioning areas among them, so that each covers a single topic or theme. If they're an ethical and professional team, they will have met well in advance of the interviews and decided on the competences (sometimes called competencies) to be adduced and the relative weightings to be attributed to each.

It may, for example, be vital to prove, if you're going for a consultancy post as a cardio-thoracic surgeon, that you have done several by-pass operations and inserted dozens of stents in patients, whereas it may be less pivotal to prove you are a good strategic thinker. The panel may heavily weight the practical experience, laying a lighter weight on the strategic thinker, even though the latter would contribute to the day-to-day running of the hospital. If, on the other hand, you're going for a post as head of cardiology, strategic thinking may be more heavily weighted, as may people management, since it is the running of the entire department which is in question.

Most experienced panels have a deep understanding of employment and equality legislation and how it relates to the questions they may ask. They may *not* ask a female candidate, for example, how she plans to manage the childcare issue her eight offspring represent.

At the outset, the chairperson will introduce the members of the panel by name and title or function. It can be quite difficult to capture all this information under pressure, so a little advance research helps. Some organisations are happy to give the names of the interviewing panel in advance. In other organisations, it becomes an open secret, even if it's not officially communicated. And sometimes, just having a word with the receptionist while you wait will give you not only the names and titles of the interviewers, because the receptionist may have them on their computer or a sheet of paper on their desk, but even where each is likely to sit.

Every moment spent waiting for an interview should be put to good use. Not so long ago, a young man looking for a job in Carr Communications, when asked the easy opening question, 'Why do you want to work here?' smilingly referred to our friendly informal atmosphere.

'Because I was so anxious to be on time,' he went on, 'I was parked in your car park three quarters of an hour ago. One of your staff stopped, knocked on my window and said, 'Why don't you come in out of the cold – we can put you in a quiet room with a cup of coffee and *the Irish Times,* if the papers have arrived.''

One way or the other, apply the rules in Chapter 3 to help you learn the names of the panel members, because it does help if you learn them and use them correctly. Ask for them to be repeated if necessary. Nobody has ever been insulted by hearing their own name reiterated.

You should use names when you can without sounding phoney. One of the best ways, when facing a panel of interviewers, is to use names when linking what is being said now to what was addressed earlier.

'Mr Nicholson touched on this, and perhaps I can link what he asked then to what Mr Roche is putting to me now…'

Or: 'This issue has a bearing on what Dr Gormley asked me

earlier…'

This method of answering is not about flattering the individuals. It's about showing you listened, and creating a community of interest between you and the panel.

Never use an interviewer's first name, even if he or she uses yours, and particularly if you know them.

You should be aware that not all the people who do personnel interviews are trained in the proper techniques. I have sat on interview boards where the members of the panel did more talking than the applicants. The applicants who did best in this situation were the ones who listened respectfully until the panellist was finished whatever he or she was saying. The applicant then came in, using their input as a platform to get to whatever point they needed to make. Applicants who fail to come to terms with talkative panellists tend to go into panic mode and try to talk the interviewer down. It never works, no matter how impatient the rest of the panel may be with the talker. You should never interrupt either an individual interviewer or a member of an interviewing panel.

If you make a mistake and notice it, ask the panel's permission to go back and readdress the question. Failure to do this has two consequences:

- You've left a wrong impression with the panel.
- You spend the rest of the interview looking back
  at the mistake, which is likely to precipitate you
  into making more errors as you proceed.

Sometimes, of course, people make mistakes and don't notice them at all. On one interview panel where a group of us were interviewing for the position of public relations officer for a state-sponsored body, one of the contenders, an enthusiastic young teacher, was asked what her first priority would be, if she were appointed.

'If I got the job,' she told the panel, 'my top priority would be to mount the chief executive on every available platform.'

The ambiguity of her statement never occurred to her, but it caused some members of the panel enormous difficulty, because they wanted to laugh.

Throughout a panel interview for a high-level post, it's worth checking that you have answered the question adequately, by asking the questioner if that was the intent of their question.

Towards the end of many interviews, the interviewer (or the chair of the interviewing panel) may ask you one of two questions.

The better of the two is this: 'Is there anything you haven't been asked that you wish you *had* been asked?'

Sometimes, this takes the form of an invitation to add anything you feel would be relevant. Consider the question. Then either tell them that you believe the interview has been comprehensive and rigorous and that you don't have anything you need to add – or offer, clearly and decisively, the extra information you want them to have, with a succinct explanation as to why you believe it to be relevant to their process.

The other question tends to be a variation on: 'Before we let you go, are there any questions you'd like to ask us?'

The honest answer may be that there's nothing you want in life, at this stage, other than to get the hell out of there and get outside a stiff gin. But if you shake your head, it tends to appear as if you have no interest in their company. At higher-level interviews, failure to ask an intelligent question at this point may amount to a seriously missed opportunity. Not because of the information you would gain, but because you have turned down a chance to relate to the interviewers as possible colleagues. It's not difficult to come up with a question based on what has been covered in the interview: 'I noticed you've asked me a lot about European languages. Would I be right in assuming that the European market is of increasing importance to Company X in the coming decade?'

('Company X' is where you insert the name of the company interviewing you. Calling it 'your company' is inadvisable, as it suggests they're just one in a line of nameless firms to which you've tossed job applications. Differentiate and individuate.)

It may also be appropriate to ask strategic questions: 'Is the thrust of your developmental plan based on acquisitions or is it more organic?'

The one thing you must *not* do is ask questions that are just about your needs. When you go into a job interview, only the employer has needs, and you're there solely to meet those needs. The final question is not an invitation to get into negotiation about terms and conditions. That's for much later.

So don't ask them what they're going to pay you. Not only is the timing wrong, but in some companies that pride themselves on the way they take care of their employees, it can result in a rejection, because they feel you do not understand their corporate culture if you think you might need to ask about money. The implication for them is that you don't trust them to treat you properly.

Sometimes, interviewees ask the panel when they'll be making their decision and when the interviewee can expect to hear from them, in the mistaken belief that this will help the panel or the interviewer realise how much in demand the interviewee is: *Hey, I have lots of other offers, you know, I can't be kept hanging around.* It doesn't work.

When the interview is over, thank the panel, but do not characterise the interview by describing it as fair. That's not your place. Just thank them and get out.

But even when you've left their premises your job is not over. Not if you want the experience to contribute to your growing communications skills. As soon as you can, whether in your car or in the nearest coffee shop, plant yourself with a computer or notebook and write down:

- Everything you were asked, in sequence
  (insofar as you can remember)
- Everything the interviewer said
- Everything you said
- Anything you planned to say but forgot

This exercise has at least four beneficial outcomes:

1. If you have genuinely forgotten to tell the interviewer something they should know about you, you can e-mail them a note about it *if this does not break the rules of the process.*
2. It allows you to plan for a second interview, if recalled. Knowing what you were asked, first time around, and what examples you provided on that first occasion can be immeasurably helpful in your preparation for a follow-up interview. Six out of ten people do worse in their second interview than they did in their first, because all they have left is spent bullets.
3. It will allow you to assess your performance and to prepare for another interview with quite a different company. The notes you take after an interview give you the evidence to work with a consultant or a trusted friend, ensuring that the next interview shows you in an even better light. It removes the possibility of making a pointless general judgement about yourself – 'I'm just no good at job interviews' – and facilitates personal growth. You're not going to blame yourself. You're going to take a detached view of yourself, as if you were a third party, and view this interview as a rehearsal for the one you will do twice as well some time in the future.
4. In the unlikely event of the interviewer or panel have treating you unfairly, the note-taking gives you a contemporaneous record you can bring with you to the management, to the Employment Equality Authority or to an employment lawyer, should you decide to protest the panel's decision.

(*Note:* Many of the rules of preparation given in Chapter 14 regarding media interviews apply to job interviews too.)

THE DOS AND DON'TS OF JOB INTERVIEWS

Do: Ask for help from within the employing organisation, if it's acceptable to do so. If you have a friend who works there, ask him or her about the company and its practices.

Do: More than obvious research. Any fool can play back to an interviewer items from the company's website. If, however, you can quote something the CEO said in a newspaper interview a year ago, or can refer to something a management guru said in a book about them, this gives more texture and traction to your comments.

Do: Dress as you would if you already held the post.

Do: Turn up in plenty of time. It's much better to be there half an hour early than two minutes before the interview is due to start, not least because an earlier candidate may have fallen off the schedule, and it will give the panel a positive view of you if you can start on time or earlier.

Do: Bring spare copies of your CV. You may need to have one in front of you as you talk, if they do the 'take you through your CV' routine.

Do: Bring a pad and a pen, if you know that writing down names or the details of a complex question will help you perform better. It's also acceptable to bring notes of points you may need to make. Just be sure they follow the same rules as notes for use in a TV studio (see Chapter 14).

Do: Look after your own comfort. Because you are likely to be nervous, your mouth may be dry. Failure to ask for a glass of water or to say 'yes, please' when they offer you a cup of tea will add to this discomfort and make you less fluent. If you want to visit the loo during the time you're waiting, don't be shy about finding where it is.

Do: Make sure you're audible. Hearing deteriorates with age, so older interviewers, even if they're not actually hearing-impaired, may hear you less easily than they might like.

Do: Say you don't know the answer to a question if you don't. The alternative is to *prove* you didn't know the answer.

Do: Answer the question – *and more than the question.* It's not a police interrogation or a quiz. Getting a correct reply back isn't the objective. Link your answer to something you want to offer.

Don't: Behave as if this was an oral exam, where they were going
to test your general knowledge or make you prove you'd
done your homework. It's an *exposition:* an opportunity to
exhibit and exemplify your strengths and competencies.

Don't: Say, 'That's a good question.' Or: 'I'm glad you asked
me that question.' In the case of the first, it's way out of
line for you to comment on the quality of the incoming
question. In the case of the second, you should be shot.
As should anybody who ever voices this stinker.

Don't: Plead for sympathy. Telling an interviewer you're nervous
is a sympathy plea. Everybody going for the interview,
to one degree or another, is nervous. Belt up about it
and don't try to make yourself seem especially fragile
or sensitive. They may decide you're too goddamn
fragile and sensitive to be employable by them.

Don't: Badmouth your present employer or boss or colleagues.
Or any from your past. The inference logically made by
the interviewer is that if you'd bitch about them, you'd
bitch about his or her firm a year or so down the line.

Don't: Behave as if they were out to get you. For them,
this begs the question: have you done something
that would justify them being out to get you?

Don't: Repeat the wording of an accusation. Think about the
question and answer it. Repeating the wording of a
negative question simply makes it more memorable
for everybody present, which isn't what you want.

Don't: Leave anything unexplained. If, for example, you
currently work for one of those multinationals that refuses
to give warm and encomiastic references to anybody,
contenting itself with a form note which confirms only
that you worked for them from this date to that date
and that your title was X, make sure, before you leave
the interview, that the recruiter knows, in advance of
receiving such a non-reference, that its brevity does
not reflect on you but is standard corporate practice in

the company wherein you are currently employed.

Don't: Carry a container-load of impedimenta. This tends to affect women more than men. Women should not carry a handbag and a briefcase and a set of keys and a mobile phone and a folder. One of the unasked questions in most job interviews is: 'Are you organised?' Dropping your keys as you walk across the floor to the board table where sit the interviewers, spending several minutes placing your belongings alongside or in front of you when you sit down or having your mobile phone play Dido's 'White Flag' in the middle of the interview tends to send a resounding 'No' to that question.

Don't: Tell them you're pleased to meet them. Say, 'How do you do?' Or, 'Thank you for seeing me.'

Don't: Employ tacky trick answers. Like, when asked, 'Where would you like to be in five years' time?' responding with self-regarding cheekiness, 'In *your* job.'

10

COMMUNICATING IN THE WORKPLACE

'Kindly let me help you or you will drown,' said
the monkey, putting the fish safely up a tree.

Anon, describing the ultimate control-freak

You get selected. You get appointed. You start the job. You live happily ever after. Right?

Not if you don't communicate well, you don't. Even if you are technically able, diligent, punctual and tick all the performance boxes, you may not survive the trial period, never mind make a success of your career, if you fail in the communications stakes.

Eighty per cent of firings, demotions and failures to promote can be attributed to communications failure. The problem is that in most workplaces, when the word 'communications' or the phrase 'communications skills' are used, they're automatically taken to refer to making presentations. Everybody agrees that everybody should communicate well but annual reviews that tell an employee that they need to brush up on their communications skills are often so vaguely couched that the employee has no clue what's really meant.

Sometimes, what is meant is that the person doesn't listen. They know it all, they finish everybody's sentences for them, they instruct others to, 'Get to the point, would you?' or, even more rudely, interrupt when someone else is outlining something with a curt, 'And your point is?'

Failure to listen blocks up information at source and information, in careers terms, is power. It also trips up the employee who *thinks* they've got the brief right, but who then miss out on some of the details. If your listening skills have been criticised, revisit Chapter 2. Or go on a good listening skills course and put what you learn into action every day.

Sometimes, an employee may listen attentively, but *negatively.* They're braced for battle long before the briefing is over. They see personal criticism in every statement. They can immediately tell anybody who suggests there's a better way of doing something that it would not apply to their department or section, that it has been tried before and failed, that they are way too busy to take on any extra tasks.

For a year, I coached a highly qualified business executive who had this problem. She telephoned me constantly to get my views on the latest outrage presented to her in the office. I had to get her, every time, to analyse the issue so that she could eventually realise that the proposal or comment was in no way outrageous.

She was like a seagull with no oil in its feathers: always in danger of being drowned by a wave that would have knocked not a feather off a normal seagull. Where her problem came from was outside my control. (We offer training and coaching, not therapy.) I had to help her understand that she had a frankly dysfunctional approach to anything anybody said to her at work. (God alone knows what she was like at home; I had to hope her husband had a particularly resilient sense of humour.)

Her dysfunctional approach took the form of a number of habits, including:

GENERALISING
'This always happens to me.' 'Nobody can stand me.'

SELECTIVITY
'It doesn't matter that the new boss says my area is one of the most important in the business, what actually matters is that he said he hoped I'd get better at working with a team. He thinks I'm useless.'

CATASTROPHISING

'I can't take this. I'm going to have to resign. There's no way out. But if I leave this job, they'll never give me a reference and I'll never get another job.'

MINIMISING

'It's irrelevant that they gave me a bonus; that was just because everybody gets one. It doesn't mean they value me, because they don't.'

CONSPIRACY THEORISING

'You don't understand the politics in this place. My assistant spends half his time playing golf with my boss and he's really clever. He gives you the impression he's on your side, but you couldn't trust him. He's very ambitious so what he has probably decided is that if he sticks it out for another few months and licks up to the boss, that's the way to get my job.'

PLAYING THE ALL OR NOTHING GAME

'If they don't appoint me to that team, it means they've decided I'm going nowhere and I'll have to get out. No, I couldn't stay if they left me out of it. Everybody would be talking about me and it would be too embarrassing to keep going.'

If you don't share any of this executive's habits of mind, your immediate instinct would be to tell her to get over herself. The problem was that she *couldn't* get over herself. Every now and then, she would have a moment of insight during which she realised how unproductive her mindset was. But it was *her* mindset and, while she could make the intellectual decision to change it, in reality, she couldn't. The voice we all have in our heads – that little mental commentator that gives us a cheer when we do something well – was, in her case, always predicting disaster, failure and extinction.

The solution lay, not in psychoanalysing her or thumping her (although the latter was an ever-appealing urge) but helping her to develop new communication skills. She agreed, first of all, to focus on the other people in her office rather than on herself, and to find out what made them tick. One of the other women turned out to be a member of a choir and when the self-punisher asked her questions about it, invited her to a concert at which she was singing. The self-punisher, who figured the other woman to be an enemy, was so flummoxed it took her several minutes to get around to thanking her colleague for the invitation.

After she'd attended the concert, she asked the other woman questions about the music and about the travel involved, reporting all this information to me as if she was transporting sand on a shovel: *Here it is, I don't know why you want it.*

She never came to grips with the principles behind her improved communications skills, never understanding, for example, that trust between human beings is built up through sharing personal details and responding to interest on the part of another person. That didn't matter. At the end of the year, she had a series of communications habits she wheeled into action every day:

- Find out something new about at least five colleagues today.
- When someone gives you a piece of advice, thank them for it.
- When someone asks you to do something differently, say, 'That's interesting – tell me why that would improve things.'
- When someone gets a promotion or task you wanted: a) congratulate them warmly; b) offer them any help you can; c) tell someone else why they were a good choice.
- When someone compliments you, thank them and show how delighted you are. Then tell someone close to you about the compliment. And about nothing *other* than the compliment.
- When someone gives you feedback, make notes of everything said. Thank them for the positives and ask for their advice in addressing the negatives. Then address the negatives, behaviourally, every day, instead of announcing that you're going to resign or be fired.

- When new ways of doing something are proposed, don't say, 'I can't do that unless you gave me X.' Say, 'One of the things that would help me do that would be X.'
- When you want to argue, don't.
- When you want to fight, don't.
- When you want to cry, don't. In any of these circumstances, go out for a walk and bring back beakers of coffee for yourself and for the person you wanted to argue/fight with or cry at.
- Don't start any sentence, in person or in writing, with 'But…'

At the end of the year, my client had a checklist she could work off and a markedly better reputation within her company. She was not a 'natural' communicator. She was like a driver who learns on an automatic car and who, put into a stick-shift, is always going to be challenged. She knew how to deal with recurring challenges in her own situation. Would she, faced with an unprecedented challenge outside that situation, be able to emotionally extrapolate from what she did at work and apply it to the new situation? I doubt it. But she was nonetheless more skilled and more effective, in communications terms, in the day job.

She also felt more in control. This is not just a good feeling. Psychologist Judith Rodin at Yale University has demonstrated how merely feeling in control can enhance the way someone's immune system works. It's one of the key factors, not just in keeping us healthy, but in contributing to our happiness at home and at work. Feeling in control comes up again and again in studies as one of the traits most often found in happy people. Paying more attention, even in a fairly ritualised way, to her communication with others widened her point of view. And, as Marshall McLuhan once commented, 'A point of view can be a dangerous luxury when substituted for insight and understanding.'

Poor communication in the office can sometimes be a symptom of control-freakery. The control-freak manager may not be a bad communicator in tone or intent. He can be the most affable, agreeable person in the world. But he can never simply brief a colleague and leave the colleague to get on with doing the job. A thought strikes him as he's on his way back to his own desk, and he returns to the fray.

'D'you know a useful guy to talk to on this would be Jason,' he tells the colleague.

The colleague agrees. Yes, Jason, known to the two of them, would probably be helpful. The control-freak goes back to his desk and a minute later his colleague's mobile phone squawks that it has a message.

'Jason will be in the office @2.'

I knew that, the colleague thinks. But fine.

'Tnx,' he texts back.

Another squawk.

'Jason doesn't need to know the budget details.'

That dumb I wasn't planning to be, the colleague thinks. Twenty minutes later, when he opens his e-mails, there's a (genuinely) helpful communication from the boss, suggesting a particular approach to the meeting with Jason.

Good communicator, that boss. Uses the technology. Moves at the speed of light. Except that what he's actually doing is *over*-communicating. The colleague he's bombarding with input is being prevented from doing his own thinking. Prevented in two ways. His boss's Niagara Falls of messages are a constant interruption to his thinking process, and over time he learns that, since his boss is going to do the thinking for him, he really doesn't need to do it for himself, which stunts his potential if he stays in that job. He also learns that, since his boss is going to remind him of every deadline and implication of every action he was about to take anyway, he can afford to get a bit sketchy on the details himself.

Meanwhile, his boss's boss is going batshit because the man in the middle, who's so helpfully communicating with everybody, is always on the verge of being late with documents for the board and can't spare the time to visit other businesses which would widen his framework or attend courses which would bring him up to speed on regulations the business must now comply with.

Over-communication and control-freakery are two sides of the same coin. But how do you find out if you're an over-communicator? Easy. Ask the people you work with. Ask them casually. Ask them over a glass of wine late Friday evening after a particularly good week at the office. But ask them. They'll tell you. They'll hedge it about with compliments – it's really nice to hear from you so often, it's great to have a colleague who's always looking out for you – but they'll tell you.

The constant availability of the means of communication
tends to disimprove the quality of communication.

How's that for a new precept? It's true. Easy access to PowerPoint disimproves the communication in 80 per cent of the situations into which it is introduced. The mobile phone allows people to be ever-present to each other while not saying anything of importance. Worse still, the mobile phone is such an *exigent* technology that people feel disempowered when they have to switch it off. Not only do some cellphone addicts *not* switch their phones off when they should, they actually take incoming calls when they very decidedly shouldn't. (Witness those who go to funerals and talk when someone calls them, whether inside the church or near the graveside.) The same is true of texting. Few behaviours are more offensive than the hand-under-the-desk performance of texters at training courses, lectures and meals who convince themselves that nobody can see them receiving and responding to messages.

Just because a text arrives doesn't mean it must be responded to. Not then, not ever.

Just because an e-mail arrives doesn't mean it must be responded to.

Cutting down on your e-mails and phone messages by 50 per cent could raise the quality of the communication by exactly the same percentage. It would give you the time to craft messages worth reading. It would prevent you from over-instructing subordinates and doing electronic nagging of colleagues. It would obviate CYA

(Cover Your Ass) messages where the sender is putting on record that they asked for a particular action or made a recommendation, so that if nothing comes through, they can point to their message and to its timing and go 'See? See?' It would reduce the awful jokes you otherwise might pass on. It would stop you wasting your time reading messages pointlessly cc'd to you and teach you not to cc your every thought to everybody you ever met.

One of the reasons control-freaks over-communicate is because they cannot postpone gratification. They need to know that what they want done is being done *now,* in *precisely* the way they want it done. (Or, even more dangerously, in precisely the way they would do it themselves.)

The capacity to postpone gratification is one of the essential traits of the good manager.

One of the most interesting psychological tests ever developed for children was called the Marshmallow Test. It involved four-year-olds, who were given a choice. Either they could take one marshmallow and eat it right away. Or they could stay in the room with the marshmallow for twenty minutes or so and, at the end of that time, if they hadn't eaten it, they would get two marshmallows.

When the test was conducted with a study group of small children, some of them, understandably, stuck in a room with a tempting marshmallow, abandoned the objective of doubling the treat and scoffed the one they had in front of them. A minority, however, held on to the promise of the second marshmallow and resisted the temptation to eat the first until the time was up and marshmallow #2 was handed over.

The psychologists followed up on the marshmallow children more than a decade later. What they found out about them was instructive. They found that the kids who had managed to hang on without eating the first marshmallow in order to earn the second one were more confident, more reliable, more able and more assertive than the kids who had given in and eaten the first sweet. They also found that the two-marshmallow children, when they reached adolescence, were less likely – when faced with difficulties – to quit. That wasn't the end of it. The four-year-olds who had held out against temptation were also more eager to learn and had better concentration in their teens, which in turn meant that they did better in exams. Unsurprisingly, they were more self-controlled than the older versions of the children who had caved in to temptation as four-year-olds.

The capacity to defer gratification puts someone in *real* control, whereas wanting reassurance on every stage of every process – control-freakery – gives the control-freak the illusion of control at the expense of the reality. So, if you find yourself wanting to text, call or e-mail someone 'just to check' on what they're doing, be aware that it may be over-communication and that you may be enslaving yourself to your technology, rather than using it to help you develop real communication networks that are productive over the long haul.

(By the way, if you suspect you might be a control-freak, the people who will tell you quickly and bluntly will be your family. A friend of mine once confided that his father was such a control-freak that he, as a child, assumed it was perfectly normal to spend your life being told how to do things you already knew how to do – particularly, in his case, play rugby – repeatedly and at high volume by someone who had no clue how to do them. He survived by developing a series of vaguely affirmative grunts which convinced his father he was paying attention to him while in fact he had mentally tuned the father out.)

Often, those who work with a benign control-freak don't complain, although they may joke around the water-cooler about them. However, a gentle, continuous push-back can alert a control-freak to their unacceptable behaviour, which can, ultimately, be helpful to them. Letting the behaviour pass allows it to become chronic, and chronic control-freakery, no matter how pleasantly articulated, is bad management.

When friends, colleagues and subordinates don't communicate this gentle push-back, it's usually for one of two reasons:

- The first is that the control-freak is a threatening, difficult person anyway and it's easier to let them have their own way.
- The second is that they're such a fundamentally good person with such manifestly good intentions that any resistance feels like biting the hand that feeds you.

But if the hand that feeds you prevents you feeding yourself, a few mild bites might be useful.

11

COMMUNICATING WITH DIFFICULT PEOPLE

Those who control their anger have great understanding;
those with a hasty temper will make mistakes.

Proverbs 14:29

One of the great myths of the modern workplace is that management and review systems stop impossible people being impossible.

The reality is that, like the poor, the difficult are always with us, and communicating with them is a daily necessity.

The dead-catter is one of the most difficult people to have around a workplace. That's the person with the unfailing capacity to produce a (metaphorical) dead cat every day. They arrive up to their boss's desk, tumble the problem onto it, and sit down, orgasmic at the prospect of discussing just how smelly and disgusting this particular dead cat is.

But they don't confine their dead cat distribution to their boss. They're the ones who know first about the terminal illness affecting an executive who's gone out sick. The ones who quickly get the inside story on precisely what was said at the Christmas party before one staff member gave another a thick ear by the application of a Gucci handbag. And they're the ones who sidle up to you and say, 'I feel you should know…'

Communicating with a dead-catter who reports to you tends to get complicated by your fear that if you cut them off at the knees, it will stop the flow of vital information and something dreadful will happen about which you would have been warned if you'd left the dead-catter alone. Get over that fear.

The first and simplest way to deal with a dead-catter who reports to you is to tell them, bluntly but good-humouredly, 'Don't bring me your problems. Solve them.'

Don't give the dead-catter lectures about the immorality of gossiping or the depressive nature of their constantly negative communication. Just dam up the source of dead cats directed at your desk. And keep damming up the supply. Repeat your mantra as often as it takes to retrain your dead-catter.

If you're a colleague of the dead-catter, you can do a version of the same thing. 'My bad news bucket is full up,' you can cheerfully announce. 'Unless you've got some good news for me, consider me closed down.'

'But...' the dead-catter will begin.

'No buts about it,' you'll chortle back. 'If it's not good news, I can't use it, right now.'

If the dead-catter sidles up to you with a 'You should know...' version of their deceased feline, listen to them. The first time. They may pass on a view expressed (it will inevitably be negative) about the clothes you wear, the language you use, the attitude you're assumed to have to an individual or a group, your failure to meet a deadline or something similar.

Analyse what you have heard. If it's simply gossip that curdles your insides and will make you self-conscious the next time you meet the person who reportedly said about you whatever nasty comment has now been passed on, thank the dead-catter and tell him or her that you find that kind of information unhelpful and that while you understand they passed it on with the best of intentions, not to do it again, because it upsets you to no purpose. Don't get angry. Just give a clear instruction as calmly as if you were asking them to close the door on the way out.

If the information could be useful, but should not have been passed on in the way it was passed on, thank the dead-catter and promise you'll go straight away to the person they quoted and get the full story out of them. This will put the heart crossways in the dead-catter, especially if you then deliver, and they'll be wary of bearing you dead cat gifts in future.

Never forget, when you plan your communication with the dead-catter or any other difficult person in the workplace, that you have wider responsibilities. A dead-catter or a bully or a sexual harrasser rarely confines their attentions to one person. They're likely to affect/discomfit more than you. So help other people deal with them by sharing your methods with friends and colleagues.

Manipulative people are extraordinarily difficult to communicate with, in the office and within the family. Here are two case histories of manipulative people.

CASE HISTORY ONE: CLIODNA

A middle manager in a large electronics factory, Cliodna was breathtakingly attractive, with a confiding way to her that added to her appeal. She reported to Aideen, who valued her highly and was convinced that, with an MBA under her belt, Cliodna would be worth promoting to the next level. Problem. Cliodna didn't want to do an MBA and was convinced she was worth promoting to the next level there and then.

Aideen's team leader was an easygoing bloke named Dave. One of Dave's better attributes was his habit of giving credit where credit was due. So at one of the coffee mornings the plant held each month to keep staff up to date on what was going on within the corporation, Dave told the group that a new approach to quality control had paid off and patted Cliodna on the back for it.

Aideen joined the round of applause but was slightly taken aback that Cliodna hadn't made her quality control proposal to her own direct report. However, a few days later, when it came to their six-monthly review meeting, she was impressed to find Cliodna had exceeded several of their agreed goals. Great stuff. She wrote a glowing report for Cliodna. What was interesting was that Dave, that afternoon, wandered past Aideen's work station.

'Hey, good to hear Cliodna got a great review,' he said, *en passant.*

Aideen, who hadn't completed the review report, thought long and hard and filed it, unfinished. The following week, she learned that one of Cliodna's assistants had in fact completed the two projects for which Cliodna had taken credit and that the assistant believed she had to keep this a secret from Aideen, because Aideen 'was out to get Cliodna'.

Not to that point, Aideen hadn't been out to get Cliodna. But the malicious untruth, the secrecy, the going over her head and the refusal to accept that she needed more education before she could be trusted with a managerial post, made Aideen decide that Cliodna was manipulative. When she challenged her on the sequence, Cliodna denied she had ever told her assistant that Aideen was out to get her. When Aideen offered to bring the assistant into the discussion, Cliodna burst into tears and explained that she was under major pressure because her mother was ill. Then she went sick and Aideen suddenly found herself encountering people from other departments who 'just wanted a quiet word' with her about her treatment of Cliodna. Aideen genially assured one of those good Samaritans, the head of another department in the plant, that if he thought Cliodna could benefit from a transfer to his (much less glamorous) area, she, Aideen, would be happy to facilitate it. He thought that was a generous and positive response and was dismayed when, on her return from sick leave, Cliodna brusquely refused the transfer. She knew when she was well off.

Eight months later, Aideen is trying to help Cliodna to play with a straight bat and not be manipulative. Whether she succeeds or fails won't be clear for some time.

CASE HISTORY TWO: ADRIAN

Adrian and Barbara started together, the same week, in a medium-sized insurance company. They didn't socialise together, but were friends. They got married around the same time. Adrian and his wife remained childless. Barbara and her husband Frank, a couple of years after they were wed, had twin sons. It was during her pregnancy that Barbara first began to suffer at Frank's hands. Or rather, at his words. He was not violent, but her changing shape disgusted him and he made no secret of it, commenting constantly and crudely about it.

After the twins were born, it got worse. His present to her after their birth was gym membership and he made it plain that he neither wanted her to breast-feed, as she had planned, nor stay the shape she was after delivery.

She went along to the best of her ability, taking extended maternity leave and then a career break because he didn't like the idea of his sons being cared for in a crèche. But full-time motherhood, combined with post-partum depression, exhausted her and despite her best intentions she found it difficult to get to the gym and even more difficult to shift the baby weight.

The following three years were hell. Meeting Adrian by accident one day in a shopping mall, Barbara, in response to his shocked reaction to the physical change in her and her obvious loss of confidence, began to cry and to tell him something of what had happened to her. He put her in touch with a therapist, and, with support from her own family, Barbara separated from Frank and won custody of the twins. When they were ten, she approached her old firm, which – at the height of the Celtic Tiger boom when good employees were hard to find – welcomed her back. Adrian, in another department, gave her the help and advice she needed to find her feet.

Going back to work was the saving of her. She went back to university at night, gained another qualification and a promotion and represented the company in radio and print advertisements.

The promotion brought her into Adrian's department, which delighted her. For a short time. Until he began to criticise her. What confused Barbara was that he criticised her for everything she thought he'd be delighted with: her confidence, the bright way she dressed, her stated ambition.

He was particularly hostile and personal at one-to-one meetings, until Barbara copped on that this was a man who liked minding women who were in victim mode, but couldn't cope with confident women who didn't need his help.

The next time he called her into his office, she brought a pad and a pen with her, and the first time he criticised her, she wrote down what he said and pleasantly asked him for a specific example of the failing he had mentioned in a general way. He flapped a hand at her and talked about something else. Sure enough, within minutes, another big general criticism arrived. Again, she wrote it down and asked him for a specific.

'What the hell do you think you're doing?' he demanded.

'Trying to improve my performance,' she responded. 'I want to eliminate the many faults you find in me and I can do that only if you give me specific examples of where those faults have shown up.'

'This meeting is at an end,' he told her.

Without ever attacking his inappropriate behaviour, she had communicated to him that it was neither right (for him as a manager) or helpful (to her) for him to make broad, sweeping, unevidenced and deeply destructive accusations. Except when he had to, Adrian stopped talking to Barbara thereafter. It didn't bother her. Partly because his silence was peanuts compared to the abuse she'd had to tolerate from Frank when the twins were small, and partly because she knew his career had plateau'd while hers was on the rise.

She did well. Constant criticism, in my view, is the most destructive behaviour employed by difficult people.

'Nothing that we encounter leads to a greater and quicker loss of control than to be criticised,' one therapist has written. 'And, equally, it is harder to retain control when we are criticised than in any other situation.'

T. S. Eliot said we should all remind ourselves that criticism is as inevitable as breathing and repetitive broad-ranging criticism shrivels the soul, no matter how often we remind ourselves of its inevitability. By 'broad-ranging' I mean criticism which claims that we're useless in one or more complete ranges of behaviour. You know the kind of accusation:

- 'You're just completely unreliable.'
- 'You're dishonest and unprofessional.'
- 'You're just not good at communication.'

- 'You never deliver.'
- 'You have no vision.'
- 'You've never understood the dynamic of my department.'
- 'I don't see you as having potential. You're not developable.'
- 'You're utterly selfish. You never think
  of anybody but yourself.'

Any one of those critiques, delivered with authority, is like being hit with a big grey cloud. You're wet. You're cold. You're dirty. You can't see a foot in front of you. Yet, every time you try to grasp a bit of it in order to get it off you, it evaporates in your hand.

Never accept big cosmic criticisms from anyone. Not from a parent, not from a child, not from a partner, not from a boss. Quietly insist, as did Barbara, on getting specific examples of what they're alleging. If they give you a single example, ask for another. And another. They'll get defensive and accuse *you* of being defensive. To which the answer is: 'No, I want to learn where I have shown this behaviour.'

If, out of all the previous year, they can give you no more than one or two examples of the behaviour, you can then quietly point out to them that one, or even two, swallows does not make a summer, and that, while you are always eager to address any failings you have, one report delivered a day late (say) doesn't justify claiming that you never deliver.

Chronic complainers will tend to back off and go to some other whinge. In which case you indicate that you tackle problems better in single file than in battalions and you'll deal with the second whinge some other time.

Afterwards, you need to remind yourself, rather than the other person, that any fool can criticise. Very few people can create but anybody can be a critic. And most critics – even the best critics – can get it grievously wrong, on occasion. Like, for example, the critic who, when the musical, *Annie Get Your Gun* opened on Broadway in the mid-1940w, said that 'Irving Berlin's score is musically not exciting or even tuneful.' (The score included hits like 'There's no

Business like Showbusiness' and 'Anything you Can Do I Can Do Better'.)

Finally, use your friends. No, I don't mean share your miseries with them. Share your miseries at work with the smallest group of the most discreet people you know, ideally a partner or best pal or mother. What I mean is make sure to pick friends who don't chip away at your confidence. If your self-esteem is being assaulted in the workplace, the friends you need are the ones who think you're mighty and have no problem telling you so.

Dealing with difficult people is easiest when they're obnoxious north-northwest: in other words, when they're consistent in the way they behave. Volatile changeable people are difficult to manage and difficult to communicate with. Particularly if they're clever about the way they manage their own communication.

An outstanding example of someone with this complex approach to manipulation, conflict, competition and management was Florence Nightingale. Nightingale laid down the foundations of nursing as a respected profession, which, in itself, was a major achievement, since nursing, before her time, was dominated by poor, filthy and alcoholic women of minimal skills.

Nightingale changed all that, although some of the congregations of Catholic nuns who, around the same time, were laying the foundations for Ireland's twentieth-century healthcare system, might dispute that she was on her own in her vision and pioneering methods. They didn't do so badly, themselves.

It didn't matter. The Crimean War gave Nightingale an opportunity to put new systems into place and to put in the measurement methods which would prove that those new systems worked. Anybody who crossed her suffered, and, as her unfortunate sister later found out, it was possible to cross Florence without ever intending to and be written off as a human being as a result.

Among those who crossed her were Irish nuns who thought she emphasised cleanliness at the expense of mercy. The nuns saw tearing off the bandages from the suppurating skin of a wounded soldier who was going to die anyway as cruel and pointless.

Nightingale promptly portrayed the nuns as filthy throwbacks and got them removed from the theatre of war. She also wrote the first draft of history, so that later historians pretty much accepted that the Irish nuns *were* sloppy and unhygienic.

She wrote letters to and about generals in the British army who resisted her that overflowed with anger, frustration and personal venom. When Queen Victoria made the well-meaning suggestion that the awful smell of gangrene in the Crimean hospitals might be reduced if she, the Queen, sent over a consignment of eau-de-cologne, Nightingale's contemptuous response, in a letter she knew would be seen by the monarch, was that it'd suit the Queen better to send over a consignment of gin. Historian Trevor Royle called her a 'bossy-boots'.

But that was only in writing. In person, she was very different. The Irish nuns could not believe that she could be so overwhelmingly warm and polite to them in person and then stab them in letters to the powers-that-were.

'On the wards,' according to her biographer, Gillian Gill, 'Nightingale remained calm, cordial, and polite whatever the provocation, and was famous among her nurses for never raising her voice. This combination of strategies was extremely effective, and Nightingale's capacity as a leader awed her friends and put the fear of God into her enemies.'

The communications lessons from the Nightingale story are multi-faceted. First of all, it's important, before you get into conflict with someone, to know how well-got they are with the people who hold the ultimate decision-making power. The Irish nuns, once they realised that Nightingale had connections with the British government they, as papists, could never have, quietly withdrew. They knew there was no point in trying to fight her, and they knew that there was no point in trying to influence her. If she abandoned any aspect of her developing dogma, it would damage her sense of herself.

G. K. Chesterton once warned against trying to persuade a triangle out of being a triangle. If it was made to be a triangle, he held, you should leave it alone, because its very identity depends on its triangle-ness and you could destroy it by trying to make it just a little circular.

Although we are up to our armpits in equality, these days, when it comes to some communication, one party is immediately at a disadvantage. That's the case in hospitals, where the acutely ill patient is behind the proverbial eight ball for a number of reasons:

- They feel cat melodeon.
- They may be frightened by how bad they feel.
- They may feel guilty that some habit (drink, drugs, fags or sex) has in some way contributed to their ailment.
- They're in bed and the authority figure (consultant, perhaps) who is talking to them is standing.
- They're wearing pyjamas. (This latter alone is traumatic for people who never wear PJs. There's nothing like a pair of stripey flannel pyjamas to reduce the self-esteem of even the most arrogantly confident man.)

Never underestimate the loss of authority consequent upon having to look up in order to communicate. It was no accident that in swash-buckling movies, the swordsman who leaps on the table is the one who can defeat three or four fighters operating from floor level.

I had a friend, recently, in that position. No, not the sword-fight position. The hospital bed position. After a severe heart attack.

Two days after the attack, he was in an intensive care bed when a specialist arrived to talk to him.

'Going to have to do a bypass on you,' the specialist told him, before giving him more detail than he ever wanted to know about this form of sophisticated plumbing.

The patient sank back in the bed as the specialist left, considering how sick he'd be after the bypass. About an hour later, another consultant pitched up beside him.

'We're going to put stents into you,' the consultant announced.

'Not a bypass?'

'Oh, no, stents are by far the best option.'

This put my friend in much better humour and gave him the courage to tell the consultant, forcefully, that, no, he did *not* want to hear any descriptions of the thrills the surgeons would have while inserting stents into his cardiac area. The consultant went off in a bit of a sulk and my friend went to sleep.

When he woke, a third consultant was standing by his bedside, amending his chart.

'We're going to control your condition by medication,' this consultant stated, hanging the chart back in its place.

'Not stents?'

'No.'

'Not a bypass?'

'No.'

'I was told by two of your colleagues that I was going to get first a bypass and then stents. Now you tell me I'm going to get neither. This,' my friend said sourly, 'this must be what's called a multi-disciplinary team in action.'

The precision of his communication, hampered though he was by breathlessness and pain, floored the consultant, who had the grace to apologise for the contradictory messages he and his colleagues had delivered, and to promise that all three would appear in the morning, clear and united on whatever decision they had made. The following morning, the patient learned that he was due for a bypass, which he duly underwent with great success a week later.

The difficulties of communicating within a team – and the potentially lethal consequences of putting a bad communicator in charge of a team – were shockingly revealed by a group of Harvard Business School researchers who usually study learning curves in semiconductor manufacture or aeroplane construction.

This research team decided to follow eighteen cardiac surgeons and their teams as they came to terms with a new technique of minimally invasive surgery. It was an interesting proposition. Teams in healthcare have to learn, change, adapt and communicate all the time in life-and-death situations, but not that much research had gone into how teams actually do it.

The phrase 'minimally invasive' makes the surgery sound easier than the traditional assault heart surgeons make on a patient's chest, sawing through his or her breastbone and pulling apart the rib cage to get at the heart. In fact, it proved to be much more difficult.

The new technique required the surgeon to operate through a small incision between the patient's ribs – so small an incision that the tubes and clamps normally used for the purpose of rerouting blood to the heart couldn't fit. So the surgeons had to learn a trickier method, requiring them to introduce catheters and tiny balloons into blood vessels, starting at the groin. This technique is now standard practice throughout the world but when it was first introduced, it meant not only that the surgeon had to develop quite a new set of skills, but that the nurses, anaesthetists and perfusionists in the team had to master new skills and roles.

At the start of the learning curve, it was obvious that the teams were coming to terms with a major challenge: they were slower than they would have liked to be, taking on average three times as long for their early cases as was ideal.

What fascinated the researchers, however, was how the speed at which the different teams learned the technique varied. They found what were described as 'striking disparities' between the learning speeds of teams in different hospitals.

Now every one of these teams was collectively expert. They all came from highly respected hospitals. Those hospitals had adopted innovative procedures before. Each team underwent precisely the same three-day training programme. Yet, when the researchers analysed the first fifty operations done by each team, they found that some teams managed to halve their operating time – and others, at the end of their first fifty cases, were still as slow as they had been at the beginning.

This finding had serious implications, not least for the patients, since slowness on the part of a cardiac team lengthened the time their patient was on support machines and under general anaesthetic, which can lead to post-operative complications. It was also puzzling, since an axiom of learning in any field, including cardiac surgery, is that practice makes perfect. Except, in this case, the axiom was not being borne out.

The researchers figured that some crucial variable in the way the surgical teams were communicating in order to manage the learning process must lie behind these statistics, and they sent the only physician among them to observe the quickest-learning team and the slowest. He didn't just observe the actual surgery. He observed what happened before, during and after the surgery. And what he found was that the fast-learning team had quite a different approach to that taken by the slowest-learning team.

The surgeon leading the team that was learning more quickly and steadily reducing the time it took them to complete the operation picked team members with whom he had worked well before. In other words, he picked people he knew, trusted and could communicate easily with. Then he kept that team intact through the first fifteen cases. No new members were admitted to his team during that period.

In briefing his team, he didn't just talk them through the procedure. He had them do through a dry run before the first case, then slated not one but six operations in the first week, to ensure a critical mass of learning. He was getting people up to speed and making sure nothing would be forgotten, as it would have been if there had been bigger gaps between operations.

But he did a lot more than that. He gathered the team before each case to discuss it in detail. After each surgery, he pulled them together to share insights about what had happened. He had the results tracked carefully and fed into those discussions. Although he self-evidently had a precise picture of what he wanted to achieve and how he wanted it achieved, the final characteristic the physician from the Harvard Business School Research group noticed he had was that he was a listener.

'The surgeon needs to be willing to allow himself to become a partner [with the rest of the team] so he can accept input,' the surgeon told the researcher.

When the physician went to observe what was going on at the slow-learning hospital, he found a very different picture. There, the surgeon – who, incidentally, was a much more experienced surgeon than the man I've just described – chose his operating team at random and let them disperse after each operation. He used a group rather than creating a team, doing the first seven surgeries with different nurses, anaesthetists and perfusionists every time. They came, they saw and they operated. Slowly.

The surgeon did not pull the members of his constantly-changing 'teams' together in advance for discussion; nor did he meet them afterwards to hear what they had learned or share results with them.

The Harvard Business School study proved that putting a group of people together under a forceful leader may look like a team and quack like a team, but it *isn't* a team. It's just a group of talented, skilled and knowledgeable individuals. To create a team requires communication. It requires that the leader, no matter how experienced or expert they are, must exercise that first essential communications skill of listening. It requires that people observe, are capable of describing what they have observed, and are surrounded by others who are eager to hear and learn from their observations. And it requires that data is explained in a way that makes sense to people at different levels of experience and expertise.

As a management consultant specialising in communications, I worry that putting people in groups and dubbing them a team often creates an unjustified expectation that the individuals within that group will communicate better within the group, whereas in fact, the group can end up glossing over the poor communications of their most difficult member.

In any area of human endeavour, this is problematic.

In medicine, it can be lethal.

Finally, on the subject of communicating with difficult people, is the single most difficult person anybody has to deal with in the course of their job: the person with a complaint. The person who is outraged by some wrong our company did them – or that they believe our company did them. They're mad as hell and they're not going to take it any more. And it's you who has to deal with them, in person or on the phone.

The first decision you have to make, in that situation, is to view the complaint as a free gift. Good companies learn more from complaints than they ever do from market research. Good responses to a complaint create customer loyalty as does no other action on the part of a firm. Dealing well with an aggrieved customer is an opportunity to put the values of your company – and your own personal values – in play in a way which can be an enormous boost to the internal pride of an organisation.

Approaching the issue in that light helps. As does putting yourself in the position of the complainant. Anybody who takes the trouble to complain is untypical. Most people who are annoyed by what a company has done to them don't tell the company, but they sure as hell tell everybody else who will listen to them, doing profound damage to the image of the company in the process.

When the aggrieved person is sufficiently motivated to lift the phone, appear in person or send a letter of complaint, it's important to consider and respond to their needs, long before you deal with the specifics of their complaint.

Every complainant wants:

- To be listened to and taken seriously.
- To have someone fully understand what happened to them and why it upset them.
- To have someone acknowledge the facts and their understandable reaction to the facts.
- They want the complaint dealt with as a matter of urgency. Any postponement or sense of casual 'We'll get to that in due course' will exacerbate their sense of mistreatment.
- They want to be dealt with as an individual, not to feel they are being shunted into a process that applies to everybody.
- Above all, they want to be treated with respect.

Down the line, they may want compensation, an apology or to get someone fired but at the outset those are their prime needs.

Before you take a phone call or meet a complainant, get all the information you can. Starting with their name. Greet them respectfully. Especially if the complainant is an older person, don't greet them by their first name. Use Mrs or Mr.

Don't use formulaic introductions like, 'I believe we have a problem?' Mrs Goggins believes *she* has a problem caused by *you* and she's not going to wear any suggestion that the two of you are on the same side. Tell her you've been told there's something wrong and ask her to tell you the details. If she's in front of you, make sure you have a pad and a pen with you and sit poised to make notes.

Don't make a speech at her. Don't tell her:

- This is the first time anybody has complained about this.
- We pride ourselves on our good service to customers.
- I will make sure everything gets sorted.

Just shut up and listen and make notes. Get the chronology right.

'Sorry, Mrs Goggins, did the spitting come before or after the bad language?'

Don't be in a hurry. Remember, Mrs Goggin's first unspoken need is to be listened to and taken seriously. When we listen seriously, we *register* what is being said.

So take the time to consider what she's saying. You don't have to comment or do dramatic indrawn breaths or shake your head in outrage. Just listen, capture, reflect. Under pressure, most of us feel the need to fill the air with noise. Don't. Fill it with respectful and silent listening.

Nor do you have to interrogate her. Complainers rarely arrive at the company which has offended them without first articulating what has happened to them to a relative or friend. Indeed, it's the reaction of the relative or friend that may have empowered the complainant to actually make the complaint. Even if it wasn't the precipitating factor, having made the complaint out loud to a third party serves as a kind of rehearsal, ensuring that by the time they get launched in front of you, they know their story. So you may not need to help them along by much questioning.

SHE'S SUCH A GIRL...

They can't say it out loud but many men find it much more difficult to communicate with women than with men. Let's be honest. Some of us women find it easier to communicate with men than with women.

It's possible to make a number of generalisations about the differences between male and female communication without going to the full extent of the *Men Are From Mars, Women Are from Venus* theories:

* Men can have a knock-down, drag-out verbal
  fight with each other, then pick up and go on as if
  nothing had happened. *Women find this difficult.*
* Men are comfortable giving orders. *Women are not.*
* Men are direct. *Women are not always direct.*
* Men argue from data. *Women tend to argue from feelings.*

The language of business, verbal and physical, whether women like it or not, is the language of men. Over time, as women achieve positions of power and influence, this may change. But don't hold your breath. And, if you're a woman, don't disenfranchise yourself by using terms and approaches your male colleagues will dismiss as 'typically female'. Start by understanding Barbara Streisand's list of comparisons, made in her Crystal Awards speech at the Women in Film luncheon in 1986:

* A man is commanding – a women is demanding.
* A man is forceful – a woman is pushy.
* A man is uncompromising – a woman is a ball-breaker.
* A man is a perfectionist – a woman's a pain in the ass.
* He's assertive – she's aggressive.

- He strategises – she manipulates.
- He's committed – she's obsessed.
- He's persevering – she's relentless.
- He sticks to his guns – she's stubborn.
- If a man wants to get it right, he's looked up to and respected.
- If a woman wants to get it right, she's difficult and impossible.

It's outrageous. It's unfair. It's untrue. But there are ways to cope with that set of prejudices.

A BUSINESSWOMAN SHOULD...

... MAKE ANY COMMENTS, WHETHER AT MEETINGS OR OTHER ENCOUNTERS, CONFIDENTLY AND WITHOUT REFERENCES TO HERSELF

'Strategically, it makes sense to acquire that company, because…'

Rather than:

'I really feel we should think about buying that company…'

(Male reaction: *'Honey, we don't care what you feel: give us the evidence on which to make a logical decision.'*)

...MAKE INPUTS WHEN THEY NEED TO MAKE INPUTS, RATHER THAN WAITING IN THE HOPE THAT THE OTHER PERSON WILL ASK FOR THEIR VIEW

'The issue is one of solvency.'

Rather than thinking:

'He really should ask my opinion because I'm actually the financial controller here…'

Remember, there are no '*shoulds*' in management. Don't project on to another person the duty you believe (even with good reason) they should fulfill. Stay on your own side of the net and get on with presenting what you should present for consideration.

...AVOID THE KIND OF LANGUAGE THAT WOULD MAKE GRUMPY
(SNOW WHITE AND THE SEVEN DWARFS) GO: 'WIMMEN!'
'Wimmen' language is covered in modifiers and apologies:
'I'd just like to raise a question about...'
'It's probably not important, but...'

...PREVENT INTERRUPTIONS WITHOUT BEING PRECIOUS ABOUT IT
Men interrupt women more than women interrupt men, especially in
meetings. Some women contribute to this by the way they sit: with
their hands below the table, as if they were doing an oral exam. The
men present, in contrast, tend to have their hands on the table, ready
to do a 'Me next' gesture to the Chair or the physical movements that
indicate agreement or disagreement.

...NOT WHINGE OR TRY TO TEACH RETROSPECTIVE
LESSONS WHEN INTERRUPTED
This is a whinge:
     'Robert, that's actually the third time you've interrupted me
when I was trying to make an important point.'
     The 'actually' and the 'trying to' are passive-aggressive. The guy
who interrupted you will roll his eyes to heaven – metaphorically if
he is too courteous to do it physically – and the rest of the group will
think 'The point you're now gonna make better be awful brilliant,
Sunshine, because you've embarrassed all of us in your eagerness
to make it.'
     Retrospective lessons are never welcome. By anybody. They're
attempted by people who are irritated by a recurring behaviour.
     'I see you yet again failed to buy stickers for the wheelie bin.'
     Reproaching someone in plenary session may feel like a good
move because the reproacher thinks everybody else will have noted
the behaviour and approve of it being challenged. It's much more
productive to control your annoyance, wait until the interrupter
has made his point, and then go – calmly and without complaint
– to what you wanted to say. Afterwards, in private, you can go to
Robert and cheerily tell him that he may not have noticed himself

interrupting you three times at the meeting but you're sure he won't do it again, will he? Once you've indicated 'Enough, already, with the interruptions, Petal,' move speedily on to some other matter of concern to the two of you, so the point doesn't sit in the middle of the conversational path like roadkill.

...INFLUENCE IN ADVANCE

Just as no good barrister ever asks a question of a witness to which the barrister does not already know the answer, nobody should ever go into an important meeting with the intention of achieving a particular objective without having prepared the ground in advance. A few offline conversations with prospective attenders at the meeting can be enormously helpful.

...NEVER POUR THE TEA

Men can do it really well but have a lot of catching-up to do in the tea-pouring department.

...NEVER BRISTLE WHEN SOME (USUALLY OLDER) MALE EXECUTIVE APOLOGISES 'TO THE LADIES PRESENT' FOR SWEARING

Don't go all old-fashioned feminist and decide that this is a form of exclusion. It isn't. It's a habit of behaviour that comes with the best of intentions. Get over it.

...NEVER PUSH THE LINE THAT 'WOMEN BRING SOMETHING SPECIAL TO THE WORKPLACE'

Women tend to drift into the 'pink collar' areas of business: HR, marketing and PR. Ambitious women tend to get into areas like finance, logistics and supply-chain management, and they don't talk that much about work–life balance, job-sharing or 'the special insights of women'. Because they know every male present will listen respectfully while stereotyping the woman involved. Know what you *can* change, know what you *can't* change, and don't waste time on the latter because you feel you should.

...SPEAK POSITIVELY AND IN THE FUTURE TENSE

'You know, this would work well if we put X in place.'

That's positive and future tense.

'This'll never work, we tried it before and unless we had X in place...' is negative and in the past tense.

It's worth repeating:

'I can't do that unless X was in place' is a deadly negative way of saying: 'Put X in place and I'll be able to do it.'

Don't reverse to a positive through a negative. And cull all the 'Buts.' Every time you say 'But' it freezes whoever is proposing something.

'This is a strong proposal. In order to make it work, we need to examine X...' is more positive than saying 'But how...'

...BE UNAFRAID OF THEIR OWN IGNORANCE OR LACK OF CLARITY

'Chairman, I need to ask a stupid question here.'

'Through the Chair, could I ask for that to be gone through again, I got lost halfway through.'

...NEVER REFER TO THEIR OWN COMFORT LEVEL

'I wouldn't be comfortable about...'

Your comfort has nothing to do with a business meeting. Present the information/evidence to query the direction, not your personal emotional reaction.

...ATTACK THE ISSUE, NOT THE PERSON PROPOSING THE ISSUE

...NEVER TALK ABOUT THEIR CHILDREN OR THEIR CATS

12

LEARNING TO SAY NO

*If you begin by sacrificing yourself to those you love, you will
end up by hating those to whom you have sacrificed yourself.*
                                                    George Bernard Shaw

Assertiveness training was the thing-of-the-moment a few years
back. It set out to help people in the workplace say 'No' when they
were way too helpful and obliging, and were led, by their own
acquiescence, into too heavy a workload and – more seriously in the
long-term – into being the person who got dumped on, rather than
listened to.

You may be one of them: the workers who accept any and
every task, who never complain, who spend their lives trying to spin
plates. You can hear one of them in a radio ad. She's obviously a
too-obliging assistant, being barked at by everybody in her company
about this report getting out on time and the need to get a courier
right away to deliver this proposal.

In the case of the radio ad, the solution to the unassertive
assistant's problems is a vitamin supplement 'proven to combat
fatigue'. The girl in the ad sounds to me like she needs a lot more
than a multi-vitamin. She needs to develop a spine. She *definitely*
needs to develop the skill to say 'No.'

Submissiveness to the demands of others buys affection and
appreciation in the short term. Longer term, however, psychological
research has discovered that, over time, this affection and appreciation
diminish. The more assertive person – the one who dumps tasks on and
constantly asks favours of the less assertive individual – experiences

low-level guilt. This doesn't make them more appreciative of the submissive person. It makes them feel irritated with them: we tend to dislike those we have wronged.

The submissive person, while this is going on, feels more and more put-upon and exploited. Invariably, they blame the more assertive person *for a problem essentially of their own making.*

In summary, the price of nice is often poisonous resentment on both sides of the relationship.

Corrective action requires the development, on the part of the nice or submissive person, of a new skill. This skill is called assertiveness, and more nonsense has been written about it than about anything else in communication, except possibly for body language.

The biggest nonsense in most assertiveness training courses is the tripartite communication they recommend. This requires the submissive person to pick a behaviour on the part of the assertive person they want changed. Then they must embark on this little formula:

- They must describe the behaviour they want changed.
- They must describe how that behaviour makes them feel.
- They must detail the effects of the behaviour on them.

Remember that scene in *The Devil Wears Prada* where the character played by Meryl Streep arrives each morning in the office and turfs her coat on the desk of the character played by Anne Hathaway, who meekly gets up and hangs the coat in a closet? If you apply the tripartite assertiveness training approach to that recurring incident, it would work out like this:

Hathaway would halt Streep one morning.

'I want you to stop putting your coat on my desk every day,' she would say to her boss.

Hathaway would then describe how the behaviour made her feel.

'It upsets me when you throw your coat on my desk. It makes

me feel like a skivvy.'

Finally, she would detail the effects of Streep's behavior as she experienced them.

'Throwing your coat on my desk startles me, disarranges the items on my desk, causes me to have to abandon whatever I'm doing at the time and makes me look like your servant.'

You can imagine the response of the Streep character. It would start with a freezing stare and end with the American equivalent of a P-45.

The theory behind the approach is that as long as you use non-judgemental language about the behaviour in the first statement the person can't get offended. Thus, because Hathaway didn't say, 'I want you to stop tossing/flinging/abandoning your bloody coat on my effing desk every shagging day,' Streep will be happy as a clam. No, she won't. Streep's the boss and believes it's her God-given right, not to say an inescapable part of her dominant behaviour in the workplace, to throw her coat wherever it suits her to throw her coat.

The theory goes on to state that expressing your feelings about the activity gives insight to the other person they may not, up to now, have had. Oh, right. Streep believed that Hathaway *loved* having coats thrown at her?

Finally, says the theory, the consquences of the behaviour should be given in order to give a full understanding to the perpetrator that what they do has an impact they may not have realised. Like Streep *cares* about Hathaway's disarranged desk.

This kind of assertiveness training has earned experts millions and generated a library-full of books on the topic. I've yet to find any objective study which proves it works. But I've come across endless examples of where it not only has *not* worked, it has worsened the situation – as does any ritualised, formulaic approach to human communication.

The first essential of genuine assertiveness is to develop personal capacity, not to set out to change other people's behaviour. Trying to change the behaviour of other people is difficult, at the best of times. Countless people go on training courses every year, for example, and – in the great phrase coined by the man in my life, Tom Savage – end up 'with bigger words for what they still can't do'.

They learn the Covey matrix (from *The Seven Habits of Highly Effective People*).

But their behaviour at work doesn't change.

They learn about how the urgent displaces the important.

But they still spend their time running from crisis to crisis instead of using their time more intelligently

Information doesn't change people's behaviour. We've all known for decades that cigarette-smoking kills people. But smokers kept smoking, and non-smokers kept taking up the habit. The single most noticeable behavior change in smokers happens after external intervention.

* Micheál Martin, when Minister for Health, bans smoking in the workplace. This leads a lot of smokers to quit and reduces the number of fags the recidivists can smoke in any one day.
* They have a heart attack, and get so scared
  that they quit and stay off the cigarettes.

It's the same in the workplace. Sending someone on a training course without putting in place a measure to assess how much they change as a result of the training course is a waste of time. At the end of every training course, the participants shouldn't be filling in daft 'smile sheets' allowing them to critique the lecturers, the food or the quality of the support documentation. They should be filling in a form which indicates how, precisely, they plan to change the way they behave in the workplace as a result of the course. Their bosses should then include the behaviour change in any review subsequently conducted.

That's what happens in pilot training. Pilots don't get asked about the presentation skills of the trainer. They get put through a set of simulations which require them to prove what they've learned.

Bottom line: changing someone else's behaviour requires that you have some power over them or that they stand to gain

in a perceptible way from the change. In an encounter between a
submissive person and an assertive person, neither factor is in play,
so the typical tripartite formula just becomes a pain in the ass to
the more assertive person, who is likely – at best – to change the
behaviour in a way which draws attention to precisely how tolerant
and responsive they are, while indicating that the demands of the
other person are demonstrative of precisely what a self-absorbed
wimp *they* really are.

Developing assertiveness should be part of your own personal
development, not a device for educating/training or manipulating
other people.

It starts with the ability to say 'No.'

Most unassertive people don't have that. When the third person
arrives at their desk to dump a task, the unassertive person smiles,
accepts and resents.

Instead, they should present data, not feelings or reproaches, to
the other person.

'Alison, you need that by Thursday. Because I have to do the
brochure for Marketing and the quarterly report for the Board, there's
no way I could get to it before Friday week.'

No complaint. No reproach. Just the facts, Ma'am.

Then offer an alternative.

'A better way to get it done by Thursday might be to give it to
Deirdre.'

Offering an alternative is good for two reasons. Firstly, it moves
the issue forward to the desired outcome. Secondly, it positions
you as more than just a dumping-ground for tasks. You become a
solutions-finder: a manager of possibilities.

Typically, the more assertive person will then resort to pleading.
Please, please, *please.*

Your response should not be to engage in a pleading response
like, 'Don't ask me, I really am under huge pressure, you know I'd
like, to do it for you, have I ever refused you before?'

Instead, repeat the data. Keep the discussion away from your
feelings and the feelings of the other person. The two of you are

colleagues trying to find a solution to a company problem.

If the other person is clever, they'll then move to flattery: they depend on you completely, you are always so obliging, Deirdre might be able to do the basics, but nobody is as good as you are at layout.

Thank them for their kind comments and don't be swayed by them. The facts stay the same: you cannot take on this task on top of what you're already committed to.

The other person, at this point, may engage in emotional withdrawal. That's a posh phrase for sulking and freezing you out. Tough. The advantage you have is that the other person is going to need you in the future. Don't comment on their emotional withdrawal and don't play into it. Keep your sunny side up and behave as if the other person wasn't sulking.

Keep in mind the instructions pilots give to passengers about the oxygen masks which may drop from overhead in the event of a change in cabin pressure. They tell you to put the mask on your own face first, before you try to assist anybody else. It makes sense. If you, as a mother, try to put the mask first on your child, you may conk out before you have it secured and have the oxygen flowing, whereas if you get the mask onto your own face first, you are in a much better position to help those around you. That's what assertiveness is all about: ensuring you are in a much better position to perform in a way that ultimately helps everybody else around you.

It's a key negotiation skill and it requires planning, each and every time, in the beginning.

That planning takes a number of steps:

* Establishing the outcome you want
* Stifling your instinctive assumption that you won't get it
* Working out the evidence that will
  persuade the other person to agree
* Talking out those points on your own
* Imagining the arguments the other person will use,
  and deciding how you should respond to each

* Removing from your language all pleadings,
  apologies and references to your feelings

This kind of preparation puts you in charge, because you have anticipated what may happen, just as a marathon-runner has worked out in their head what it will feel like when they 'hit the wall' and how they're going to cope with it when it happens in reality.

Under-assertive people, when they embark on this kind of preparation, tend to get stuck at the second point. They can produce statements of failure with appalling ease:

* 'I just know what she's going to say.'
* 'I can't bring myself to…'
* 'This won't work.'

If you cannot move beyond these statements, then don't enter the negotiation – because, quite apart from being unable to change someone else's behaviour, you're proving you can't change your own behaviour.

If, on the other hand, you disqualify all the negatives, you are training yourself to behave as if the outcome were inevitable. You are training yourself to behave as if you had more confidence than you actually have. 'Behaving as if' is one of the devices in cognitive therapy which is proven to work. If you behave as if you were confident, other people assume you *are* confident and start treating you the way they treat confident people. A positive feedback loop is established and before you know it, you're *actually* feeling more confident. The song 'I Whistle a Happy Tune' from *The King and I* is a neat example of the process, put to music.

However, acting and feeling as if you were more confident will not solve the problem of anger on the part of the other person. Anger is a deadly weapon. In the workplace, it can take the form of someone invading your space, pointing an accusing finger at you, staring you down or raising their voice. None of which is acceptable.

If someone invades your space, walk away. Get a desk or a

table between you and the person.

If someone points a figure at you, look at the finger. In astonish-ment. As if it was a sheep that had suddenly arrived in the room. The other person will get self-conscious and stop the gesture, without you saying anything.

If someone stares you down, don't look away. Examine the bridge of their nose with great attention. They won't be able to work out precisely where you're looking, but the discomfort of your not meeting their eyes will make them realise the glare's not working.

Finally, if someone raises their voice to you, *lower your own voice*. It's one of the infallible tools of conflict-management, and always drags the other person's voice down to normal volume.

Assertiveness is behaviour-with-an-objective. Not a song and dance act. Assertive people don't have to be assertive all day long. If they've nothing to achieve, there's no reason for assertiveness. Becoming more assertive doesn't mean you have to become more bossy, making inputs all the time to every conversation.

All you need to do is use assertion when it will be useful in achieving an objective.

13

Communicating Like a Leader

In getting most jobs, academic intelligence is the doorway, the entry level qualification. To become a business leader requires more than that. The people who succeed – internally – in motivating staff, and – externally – in building and developing customer loyalties, who function well in relation to stakeholders and boards of management are people who make relationships, people who are emotionally intelligent.

If you don't have emotional intelligence, your communication capacity is inevitably spavined and you'll have a short-lived success wherever you will be. Long-term success – especially if that success is a leadership role – is fundamentally related to your level of emotional intelligence. According to Tom Savage, lecturer and author of *How to Get What You Want*:

> Being emotionally intelligent means, in the first place, that you understand your own emotions and can control them and the impact they have on yourself. You're also very aware of, and sensitive to, the effect your emotions have on other people: the impact they have on them. A hallmark of someone emotionally intelligent, for example, is the capacity to tell funny stories against themselves. They can do this – comfortably recount occasions when they made mistakes – because their self-esteem is not dependent on people having a false notion of them.

The awareness of this capacity is a key development in business at the moment: the realisation that when you're recruiting people, you don't ask them general-knowledge quiz questions. You test them on those competences which make up someone who is emotionally intelligent, emotionally secure.

You can, according to Tom Savage, develop your own emotional intelligence.

> You can't do much about the genetic endowment of physical intelligence but you can certainly raise your emotional intelligence. It's not easy, depending on the heredity and upbringing you've had, but whatever the forces that have shaped you, if you decide to do it, nothing to stop you. Because emotional intelligence is inextricably tied to communication. Over the years, Carr Communications has carried out communications audits for companies. One of the sections offers thirty different factors that demotivate staff at work. Unfailingly over the years, the top one that comes out is that staff believe they are not listened to and have no voice in the decisions that shape the business. This makes no sense. Staff are the people who are at the coalface. They're at the leading edge. They're meeting the customers. They're developing the products. Nobody knows more or has more real lived experience of the product or service that the company is providing than front-line staff. Yet management will make decisions about changes, about things that are going to happen and these will be handed down to staff without the staff being involved in any kind of consultation that would make such changes realistic and viable.

Emotionally intelligent leaders have a number of common characteristics.

- They're observant.
- They're analytical, but know when to take action.
- They don't always 'go by the book'.
- They make mistakes, but still inspire.
- They don't panic.
- They use the language/imagery of the people they lead.

Not all great leaders have all those traits. But outstanding leaders demonstrate some of the traits in action.

GREAT LEADERS ARE OBSERVANT

Alexander the Great was King of Macedonia 2,350 years ago. He ended up ruling half the world. He was clever. He studied hard. He had courage.

But most of all, he *observed*. Meaning he kept his eyes open and didn't miss stuff. That showed up early in his life.

His father had a horse named Bucephalus. Big. Wild. Dangerous. Vicious. Nobody could tame the horse. Everybody was scared of it. His father had decided to kill off the horse.

And then Alexander said, 'I can tame Bucephalus.'

Because he had watched the other guys trying to tame it and had noticed something they'd missed.

The horse was terrified of its own shadow. The bright sunshine created this big, threatening shadow. When the horse reared up trying to get away from the threat, the shadow would rear up, too.

Alexander caught the horse and turned it facing the sun. So its shadow was behind it. Where it couldn't see it. Then he slipped a bit into its mouth and got up on its back. Kept it facing the sun until it got used to him. Then, when he was sure he could calm it, he let it see its shadow again – but kept talking to it. Within a couple of days, he had tamed Bucephalus. The horse became his favourite warhorse – he rode it into one battle after another. It had huge courage.

What Alexander proved was that good leaders watch. They work out how to get the best out of people (and animals). They know that encouragement can overcome fear.

GREAT LEADERS USE ANALYSIS – AND ACTION

A few hundred years ago in England, people were dying like flies of a disease called cholera. Once you got it, you threw up. Again and again and again. Within a few hours, you were shrunken and sinking into a coma.

People were terrified of cholera. Because they didn't know

what caused it. One doctor looked at the map of his town. He had the list of who had died and where they had lived.

And he began to realise – Oh, look, a hundred and fifty people died in *this* area yesterday, but only twenty people in this area.

He started to ask himself questions. Why would so many people die in *this* area? What's the cause? Maybe it was the water they were drinking. The water they took in leather buckets from a pump...

Dr Snow worked out that the people who were dying were all getting their water from one pump. Having done the analysis, he then did what good leaders do: decided to take a risk. He went out one night and took the handle off that pump, so nobody could use it. People had to drag themselves to pumps further away and drag their water back greater distances.

But they stopped dying.

Later on, when microscopes were developed, it would have been easy to discover that human waste was seeping into the water of that pump. Dr Snow didn't have the benefit of modern technology so he could not know *why* the pump was deadly. He just knew it *was* deadly. He took the risk of annoying people in order to save their lives.

GREAT LEADERS DO NOT GO BY THE BOOK

A peptic ulcer is a very painful disease, which for aeons was believed by many doctors to be the result of stress.

'You have to relax more,' they would say to patients.

Another theory was that the peptic ulcer was caused by eating spicy food.

'You must not eat curry,' they would tell their patients, encouraging them to eat bland foods and drink lots of milk.

The stress-and-spice theories were the received wisdom, and 99 per cent of doctors 'went by the book.' One didn't.

'Could an ulcer be caused by a germ?' he wondered.

He went to work in a laboratory and proved to himself that it *was* caused by a germ. A germ called *helicobacter pylori*.

Except that, when people have lived with a received truth for a long time, they are extraordinarily reluctant to relinquish it.

'Ulcer patients may have a lot of that germ in their body,' was the reaction of the doctors who preferred the traditional approach. 'But that doesn't prove it causes ulcers.'

Eventually, the doctor decided there was only one way to prove it. He drank a big dose of the germ – and immediately got an ulcer. It wasn't fun but his personal experiment changed the way ulcers are treated. He made a lot of lives easier. Because he didn't allow his thinking to be constrained by received wisdom. He didn't go by the book once he had the information which proved the book was out of date.

GREAT LEADERS MAKE MISTAKES
– AND ARE STILL INSPIRING

One of Carr Communications' trainers, Anton Savage, constantly hammers home what he calls the 'General Patton line on wardrobe'. Patton insisted that all his guys wore ties at all times and were spit-and-polished to within an inch of their lives. Not because of how it made them look, but because of how it made them *feel*: being forced to dress 'properly' every day tended to raise morale and a sense of teambuilding.

He was also a great orator. But Patton made one horrific mistake in his career. Visiting a hospital, in the middle of the war, where the wounded were being treated, he encountered an ambulant patient. In other words, a guy who wasn't stuck in a bed, missing a limb or covered in bandages. The guy looked pretty normal. Patton asked about him and was told he was suffering from 'shell-shock,' which, at the time, was how post-traumatic stress disorder was described.

The General decided this man was a coward, and smacked him in the face with the gloves he was carrying. It was a ghastly thing to do and very nearly cost him his job.

What it *never* cost him, however, was the loyalty of his troops, including the man he had slapped. Patton's capacity to be an inspiring leader outweighed his mistakes.

GREAT LEADERS DON'T PANIC

The first chapter of this book dealt with flawed communication and poor leadership causing air crashes.

The disaster in Sioux City, Iowa, in July, 1989, illustrated the opposite: good communication by a born leader who did not panic. The pilot of United Flight 232 was Captain Al Haynes. Part way through the flight, his plane, loaded to the gunnels with passengers, lost all hydraulics. What happened was that a tail engine fan disc had fallen off the plane into a field of corn. This was caused by a manufacturing flaw.

Haynes didn't know the cause. All he knew was that the plane could not be controlled. He stabilised the plane as best he could, worked through with his crew all the possibilities, then told air traffic control about his situation.

'We have almost no controllability,' he reported. 'Very little elevator, and almost no ailerons, we're controlling the turns by power…We can only turn right, we can't turn left. I have serious doubts about making the airport. Have you got someplace near there, that we might be able to ditch? Unless we get control of this airplane, we're going to put it down wherever it happens to be…Whatever you do, keep us away from the city.'

As you can see, even in a chaotic situation, Haynes was calmly taking charge, considering the dangers to city dwellers below him. In his communication with his crew, he was not only calm, he even managed to be humorous. His crew rose to his leadership, arranging the passengers so that each of the thirty children on board was re-seated beside an adult. The passengers, in turn, reacted calmly.

Haynes's avoidance of panic was helped by his instinct to find positives within a devastatingly negative situation. So, for example, he registered that he was flying over fairly flat land, which offered some chance of survival in the event that he had to ditch short of an airport.

'That relieved a lot of pressure on us, in whether or not we were going to make the airport,' he said, after the crash. 'At least we could get it on some pretty flat ground.'

Weirdly, the air traffic controller who cooperated superbly with Haynes throughout the incident had moved to Sioux City because he had found his previous duty station too stressful and was looking for something a little quieter...

Haynes credited the calmness in the air traffic controller's voice as helping his own panic-avoidance. The only thing the Captain found deeply frustrating, in the run-up to the crash, was the fact that advisers on the ground kept telling him that he couldn't be having the problem he knew he was having. He did not yell at them. He just kept repeating the facts to them.

Haynes was injured in the crash, but he survived, as did more than half the passengers. His management of the shockingly unexpected is one of the legends of air flight in its demonstration of a leader who does not panic.

GREAT LEADERS USE THE LANGUAGE AND IMAGERY OF THE PEOPLE THEY LEAD

This is arguably best demonstrated by the language used by Christ, as described in the Gospels. But St Patrick is up there, too, using a native weed, the shamrock, to explain the concept of the Trinity. So is Jesse Jackson (See Chapter 5).

14

SURVIVING A MEDIA INTERVIEW

A researcher telephones you to invite you to participate in a radio or TV chat show. Before you make the decision whether or not you should accept that invitation, use this checklist:

* Who is the audience?
* What is the topic?
* What areas are to be covered?
* What is the angle?
* Why am I being asked to speak?
* What is my interview sandwiched between?
* Who else will be on the show?
* What time will it go out?
* What time will it be recorded at, if it's not live?
* How long will the broadcast last? (Or:
  How long will the recording last?)
* Is it a panel or a one-to-one?
* Who will be on the panel?
* What position will they take on the topic?
* Is it a phone-in interview?
* Where will the interview take place?
* How much preparation time is available before the broadcast?
* How can I get there? What are the
  parking/security arrangements?

If you decide that you can reach a specific audience through the programme, you agree to go on. But only if you have enough time to prepare. *Never* accept an invitation to 'go on the air three minutes from now' by phone. You would never choose to address 500 people in a hall without preparing what to say; why should you address 500,000 people through their radios without preparation?

HOW TO PREPARE FOR A RADIO OR TV INTERVIEW

WHO IS MY AUDIENCE?

Decide who you're talking to. Never mind the general public. What's the general public to you or you to it? You can't decide exactly what you're going to say until you have decided exactly who your audience is. Your target audience will usually be a subsection of the total audience for the programme. You can guess who the audience for the programme is from the time it is broadcast. For example, *Morning Ireland* is on from 7 am to 9 am. The audience is businesspeople going to work. *Scoige and O'Shea* on afternoon television reaches people who are at home in the late afternoon, *not* business people.

WHAT IS THE AUDIENCE'S PRESENT POSITION ON THE TOPIC?

Try to put yourself in the shoes of a member of your target audience. Guess exactly what they think about your topic. If you cannot do this, chat to a few members of your target audience and work out what they are thinking about the issues you're going to address.

WHERE THE
AUDIENCE IS NOW

What they know

What they feel/believe

What Do I Want my Target Audience to be Thinking, Saying or Doing after the Interview?

You must have a communication goal. This goal is to shift the target audience from position A to position B. Identifying your audience and your communication goal are the two most important steps in preparing for a radio interview. If you get these wrong your interview will not be effective.

Don't be over-ambitious. In a four-minute interview, for example, if you're a very good talker, you might make your chosen audience remember three pieces of information. You certainly won't make them remember six pieces of information.

Preparing for an Interview Grid

When you have worked out the three pieces of information you want the audience to remember, and the emotional decision or opinion you want them to adopt, write them in the first column of the preparation grid.

The second column of the grid is about making the points memorable. In this column, list examples with specific, graphic details which vividly illustrate the points you wish to make. For each point you may wish to choose one or two vivid examples.

Let's imagine that the first point you want them to remember is that the new road will cut traffic jams.

To make that memorable, you need to illustrate it, put details into it, make the listeners draw their own pictures. Like this:

- Up to now, if you wanted to get to Bigtown from Littletown, it could take you an hour in the afternoon, but two hours at busy times. Factories in Bigtown had huge problems with workers arriving late through no fault of their own.
- Anyone who has to do the journey regularly knows that they could be sitting at the third bend, where the fire station is, for three quarters of an hour or more, inching forward every ten minutes.
- Parents found they had to get small children up at 7 in order to get them to their playgroup at 9. That's going to change.

In the third column, you list the obvious questions.

In the fourth column, you list the questions you sincerely hope you will not be asked. The stinkers.

(A quick brainstorm with colleagues will give you the contents of the two last columns.)

Now take a pen, close your eyes and aim at one of the two columns on the right. Read aloud the question on which your pen lands, and answer it, seeking to link to one of the points you want to make. With a little practice, it becomes easy to get to the items you have prepared to offer.

It's important to remember that *offering* is precisely what you are doing. You are not setting out to avoid questions or manipulate the interviewer. You are simply moving the interview from being an oral exam into being an opportunity for you to offer interesting added-value information to the listeners.

Talk your answers out aloud. Sometimes, we hear ourselves saying something which, we realise, does not do justice to the point we wish to make. It's a lot better to find that out at home or in the office, before we go to the studio, than live, on the air.

When you're sure of what you're going to offer, take a card and, with a big, black felt-tip pen, put down a few trigger words:

- Factories – workers late – no fault
- Fire station corner
- Toddlers up at 7

Make sure you also note down any figures, names or other factual data which might elude you under pressure.

When you're picking examples for a TV or radio programme, pick *visualisable* examples. The more people can rustle up a mental image of what you're talking about it, the more likely they are to engage with it.

When it comes to interviews remember:

EXAMPLES SHOULD BE SINGULAR RATHER THAN PLURAL, SPECIFIC RATHER THAN GENERAL

General truths slide off the mind. Here's one of them:

The notion of moderation is subjective.

Here's that same truth, cast in a singular, visualisable example:

One man in the study, describing himself as a moderate drinker, drinks seven pints on the average night out.

STORIES ARE IMPORTANT

Story has been the foundation stone of every culture in every country in the world at every period in its history. We love stories. We *remember* stories. So, whenever you can cast your argument in the form of a story, do so.

REPETITION IS VALUABLE

If you can come up with more than one way (in the second column on the grid) to make a point you've identified (in the first column) as essential, this is to be welcomed. They don't put TV ads on several times a night without a good reason. Advertisers know that repetition of key messages is a vital aspect of changing people's attitudes and behaviours.

WHAT POINTS MUST THE AUDIENCE REMEMBER?	THOSE POINTS INTERESTING AND MEMORABLE	OBVIOUS QUESTIONS	NASTY QUESTIONS

THE FIRST AND LAST QUESTIONS FOLLOW A PATTERN
In most interviews, the first question is: *What's the story here?*

In most interviews, the last question is: *Where do we go from here?*

Different words are used. But the meaning is usually some variant of these two questions. Prepare accordingly.

KEEPING CONTROL OF THE INTERVIEW

TALK ABOUT SPECIFIC EXAMPLES
If you talk in general terms, you're easy to interrupt and difficult to remember. Use detailed examples to illustrate your points.

YOU'RE THE EXPERT ON YOUR TOPIC
Set out to be interesting. Don't force the interviewer to ask a million questions to get the story out of you.

IF YOU DON'T KNOW THE ANSWER, SAY SO
If you don't know the answer to a question, you can either say you don't know or prove you don't know. Never prove you don't know. Say it and offer to solve the information problem as soon as you can. If you are confused by the question get it clarified.

USE FIRST NAMES RARELY
Don't try to flatter interviewers by using their first name. Once at the beginning – only. Your target audience is out there in kitchens and motorcars. If you continually use the interviewer's name, it makes the audience feel they're eavesdropping – they're outsiders.

GO LIVE IF POSSIBLE
Newcomers to radio and TV always prefer to be interviewed on tape, rather than live, because they believe it will allow their mistakes to be corrected. The possibility of pre-recording makes them feel more safe. More in control of the situation.

In fact, it's the other way around. Going live puts you in much more control than being taped. You can intervene, you can respond, you can even walk out on a live programme, whereas, once a programme is taped, you've handed everything over to the producer/ director. The producer/director is not out to get you. But they may decide that editing out point E from your input will radically improve their programme, whereas point E may, in your opinion, be by far the most important thing you want to say on the programme.

In a live programme, point E gets made.

In a taped programme, point E may end up on the cutting-room floor.

Of just as much importance is the reality that, because you know the programme is being taped, because you know it's possible to edit what is being said, the edge goes off your performance. Having to participate in a live programme gives a do-or-die urgency to one's performance which can make it much more exciting to the listener or viewer.

Sometimes, it's not possible to appear live on a programme. When that's the situation, go into the recording *as if it were live*. Remember, the programme-makers are busy and under pressure. If you make a mistake which is less than crucial, they're likely to say that it's not important and to avoid editing it out. So get it right the first time.

If you're being taped on a sensitive topic, make sure to hear or view the tape before the production team departs, and if you believe any of your answers contain correctable errors which might mislead the viewers/listeners (as opposed to containing sloppy grammar of which you might be ashamed) make sure the inaccuracy is erased and the correct data recorded before the team goes.

If your home or your office is frequently visited by TV crews, there's a case for setting up an 'interview corner' to facilitate those crews.

But always remember, if you have an option, live broadcasting is best. And if the TV crew come to *you,* have somewhere appropriate for the recording selected and cleared in advance.

THE INTERVIEW CORNER

Political parties and big companies increasingly find they need to have a designated corner in their premises where a camera crew can quickly set up to film an interview. The corner should be a right angle, with the walls on either side covered in bookshelves. Bookshelves filled with books convey a calm, pleasant atmosphere to the viewer, and they also absorb more sound than does a flat wall.

Check the titles of the books on the shelves so that nothing odd or questionable attracts the attention of the viewer. In addition, before you admit a media crew to your home or office, have a look around to see if any ornaments or pictures might inadvertently send an inappropriate message, via the camera. For example, if your company is in trouble, it wouldn't be a good idea to be filmed in front of an oil painting showing a ship sinking in stormy seas.

Two matched comfortable chairs should be in the interview corner. These chairs should not be the kind which spin – under pressure, as already stated, people instinctively engage in repetitive movements, and few are more irritating to watch than the forward-and-back action of someone fidgeting in a spinning chair.

If the production team wants to interview you out of doors, make sure your hair doesn't take partial flight in response to passing breezes. Long hair should be clipped or gelled. Another way of controlling it is to tuck it under the collar of your coat or jacket.

Even out-of-doors, you should consider what your surroundings may say about you. The visual is more important, in TV terms, than the aural. A classic example of someone failing to consider their surroundings occurred when a European chemical company had a fire. Their safety and environmental officer was interviewed by a TV reporter in front of the building. So, while he talked, a threatening column of black smoke rose in the background. That was bad enough.

What was worse was that, as he spoke, part of the plant exploded. He instinctively ducked. Nobody remembered the reassuring statement he was making. Everybody remembered the pictures.

Sometimes, TV crews like to get shots of their interviewer walking along beside the person being interviewed. In that situation, make sure you walk the distance several times in advance of the actual recording, so that it's familiar to you and you don't have to keep looking down at the terrain you're covering.

When you're being interviewed in a TV studio, don't move the chair. It has been positioned and lit before you arrive, so by moving it, you may move yourself out of optimal lighting. However, when you sit down, if you find any aspect of your location discomfiting, ask the floor manager to rectify the situation. The floor manager is the man or woman with the two-way radio attached to their belt. Their title means precisely what it says: they're in charge of everything that happens on the studio floor and can make any modifications that will help you.

Bring whatever notes you want, ideally written on yellow, rather than white paper, because it's easier to read from and reflects back less light.

Notes taken into a TV studio should be twice as big as our normal handwriting, and written by a thick black felt-tip pen, so that they lift off the page at a glance in one cognitive chunk.

Notes should be simple and indicative, rather than detailed. Writing full sentences is always a mistake. They provoke a desire to read them on air, and only newsreaders are trained for that task. Keep them simple. They should include:

- Names of other participants
- Key facts you might forget

- Figures you might need to quote
- Key words related to illustrations you want to present

The preparation grids mentioned earlier should *never* be brought into a TV or radio studio. They are for preparation purposes only, and are far too detailed and complex to serve when you are live on the air or being recorded.

Notes should be on separate pages or cards, not on flimsy paper attached by paperclip or staple. Cards should be large and few, rather than tiny and many.

When you sit down in the radio or TV studio, work out where the presenter is going to be. His or her position establishes your gaze path throughout the programme: where you'll most frequently be looking. Your notes should be in your gaze path, so that you don't have to glance away from the presenter and effectively disengage from the programme in order to refer to them.

The most important thing you will bring to the studio is *content.* What you wear is much less important. But let's help you get that right, too.

Any woman who wants to convey an immediate impression of authority is well advised to wear a tailored jacket. Research shows that if a group is shown a picture of a man in his shirtsleeves, they assume he has a jacket somewhere, whereas if the same group is shown a picture of a woman without a jacket, they assume she is a secretary.

Be wary of wearing either black or white. Black absorbs too much light. White reflects back too much light. If you want to wear a dark colour, go for navy, chocolate or charcoal. Dark colours make you look thinner on TV, which can be helpful, since, because the TV picture is delivered in horizontal stripes, it adds roughly ten pounds to everybody. Flat, thin fabrics also reduce the appearance of size, whereas thicker, textured fabrics like tweed, velvet or bouclé add volume. Vertical stripes make their wearer more slender in appearance, whereas horizontal stripes make their wearer look fatter.

The camera finds it difficult to interpret small checks, like houndstooth or Prince of Wales check, and so strobing or jiggling can happen to the picture. Avoid them.

Fabrics like satin and details like sequins should never be part of a TV wardrobe. They catch the light and distract from what you're saying. Indeed, a good basic rule for your TV wardrobe is: *Don't wear anything that's louder than you are.*

'Loud' clothing includes:

* Polka dots
* Assymetrical details
* Earrings that move
* Bangles that jangle
* Tops revealing cleavage

Badges and brooches can create their own 'noise.' For example, many women like to wear the pink ribbon indicating their support of research into breast cancer. That's fine if breast cancer research is the subject of the interview. If it's *not* the subject of the interview, eschew the badge. Wearing it will simply provide a point of disaffection: a distraction wooing viewers away from concentration upon the key points you want them to register.

Under pressure, women tend to blush. Wearing a low-necked dress or shirt can reveal blotchy redness when blushing happens. Either wear a higher neckline or make sure the exposed area is made up to conceal any emerging redness.

It can be useful, in advance of an appearance, to ask the researcher or reporter about the colour of the studio set, so that you don't arrive wearing a jacket of precisely the same colour. Indeed, bringing a spare jacket is a useful measure to obviate the possibility that another woman on the same programme may be wearing an identical colour.

Button-through shirts should be checked in advance of an appearance to make sure they don't gap at the bustline. When you've put on the shirt, sit down in front of a mirror to check if this is likely to happen. If it does, double-sided tape can be used to keep the two edges together. Ordinary double-sided tape will do, although accessory shops carry heavy-duty versions of the product which are particularly effective.

Finally, instead of white, go for pastels. A pale-blue or pale-pink shirt will provide good contrast against a dark jacket.

Even if you don't usually wear make-up, a TV station will expect to make you up before an appearance. The objective is not to prettify you but to allow the TV camera to deliver a truthful version of you to the viewer.

If you're *not* made up, your face may look flat and featureless under bright lights. More to the point, the heat from those bright lights will make you shine.

Make-up artists in TV stations are experts who love to be helpful. They will try to achieve the look you want, and should be asked about anything about which you have a concern.

Be prepared, if undertaking a lengthy recorded interview, for the make-up artist to appear, whenever there is a break, to 'powder you down'. Heat softens make-up and made-up faces go quickly from a pleasant glow to an oily sheen, so the make up artist will frequently damp down that shine with face powder.

When you're in charge of your own make-up, go for a slightly warmer shade of foundation than you normally use. If you don't normally wear make-up at all, use a foundation which is either cream-to-powder, coming in a compact with a sponge which is dampened for application, or Max Factor Pan Cake makeup, which is a water-based version of the same thing. Outline your eyebrows using light individual strokes. Powder your eyelashes and then apply mascara. Go easy with lip gloss. And have a compact of compressed translucent face powder to hand.

Rosacea affects many women in their middle years, giving them a permanent redness. (It affects men, too. Former US President Bill Clinton suffered from it.) Believe it or not, green cream underneath a normally-hued foundation corrects this ruddiness, and is available from pharmacies, make-up emporia and outlets like the Body Shop.

TEN MEDIA INTERVIEW DON'TS

1. *Don't* bring the preparation grid into the studio: it's too complicated. Bring the card. You may not need it. But it is a reassurance. And remember, keep it in your gaze path.

2. *Don't* write out full sentences on the card: radio presenters dread the interviewee who comes and reads aloud, rather than answering questions in a vivid immediate way – and the problem is that once you've written out a full sentence on a card, you develop a certain loyalty to it.

3. *Don't* say, 'I'm glad you asked me that question,' or, 'That's a good question.' Just get to your answer.

4. *Don't* tell the interviewer what to ask you. Stay on your own side of the fence and find a way to offer what you came to offer.

5. *Don't* argue with the interviewer. It's not him or her you have to persuade. It's the people at home. Think of the interviewer as a telephone you're using to get to that wider public. Nobody fights with a telephone.

6. *Don't* attack the man or woman, attack the issue. No personal insults or attacks on the organisation represented by another participant.

7. *Don't* repeat the words of an accusation. If an interviewer says 'I put it to you that your organisation has been associated with murder, rape and pillage,' responding, 'My organisation has never been associated with murder, rape and pillage,' ensures that the people listening will make the link between murder, rape, pillage and your organisation. By repeating it, you've drummed it into their minds. Instead, get to the positive.

8. *Don't* put padding in front of your answers: 'Well, it's important that your listeners see this issue in its wider context.' Cut to the chase. Get to the point.

9. *Don't* bring a mobile phone, a pen with a clicky end, a pager or a watch that tweets on the hour into a TV/radio studio.

10. *Don't* wait for the right question. It may never arrive. Find a way to make your point without it.

BIBLIOGRAPHY

Bolster, Evelyn. *The Sisters of Mercy in the Crimean War*. Mercier Press, 1964.

Cialdini, Robert B. *Influence – Science and Practice*. Allyn & Bacon, 2001.

Clark, David M. and Christopher G. Fairburn (eds.). *Cognitive Behaviour Therapy*. Oxford, 1997.

de Becker, Gavin. *Fear Less: Real Truth About Risk, Safety, and Security in a Time of Terrorism*. Little, Brown, 2002.

Gill, Gillian. *Nightingales*. Random House, 2004.

Kearns Goodwin, Doris. *Team of Rivals: The Political Genius of Abraham Lincoln*. Simon & Schuster, 2005.

Nuland, Sherwin B. *The Doctors' Plague*. Atlas Books, Norton, 2003.

Maister, David H., Charles H. Green and Robert M. Galford. *The Trusted Advisor*. Free Press, 2000.

Parrott, Les, III, *Control Freak*. Tyndale, 2000.

Prone, Terry and Kieran Lyons. *This Business of Writing*. Institute of Chartered Accountants in Ireland, 2007.

Savage, Tom. *How To Get What You Want*. Marino Books, 1999.